"CHRONICLES OF THE VERDANT WORLD: A JOURNEY THROUGH ENVIRONMENTAL SCIENCE"

ACCORDING TO PCI SYLLABUS

AISHWARYA JAIN

Made with ♥ on the Notion Press Platform
www.notionpress.com

To my dearest family, mentors, and students,

This book is a reflection of the collective wisdom, support, and inspiration that each of you has generously bestowed upon me. To my family, who has been the unwavering foundation of my life, thank you for your love, encouragement, and understanding throughout this journey. Your sacrifices and boundless support have been the bedrock upon which I've built my dreams.

To my mentors, whose guidance has been a beacon illuminating the path of knowledge and self-discovery, your insights have shaped not just the words on these pages, but the very essence of my being. Your belief in my potential has fueled my determination, and your lessons have been invaluable milestones on the road to growth.

And to my students, the vibrant souls who have enriched my life with curiosity and fresh perspectives, you are the reason I continue to learn and strive for excellence. Your enthusiasm and inquisitiveness have been a constant reminder of the profound impact education can have on shaping minds and hearts.

This book is dedicated to all of you, my cherished family, mentors, and students. May it stand as a tribute to the bonds we've forged, the lessons we've learned, and the collective strength that has propelled me forward. Your presence in my life has made this journey richer, and for that, I am eternally grateful.

With heartfelt appreciation,

Aishwarya Jain

Contents

Foreword

In the intricate web of our planet's ecosystems, where the delicate balance of nature weaves together the threads of life, the importance of understanding and preserving our environment has never been more crucial. As we stand at a critical juncture in the history of our planet, this book on environmental science emerges as a guiding beacon—a comprehensive exploration of the interconnected systems that sustain life on Earth.

Navigating the complex terrain of environmental science requires not only knowledge but also a deep appreciation for the intricate relationships that govern our natural world. In the pages that follow, the author delves into the multifaceted realms of ecology, conservation, climate science, and sustainable practices. It is a journey that beckons readers to ponder the profound interconnectedness of all living things and the responsibilities we bear as stewards of this shared home.

What sets this book apart is its ability to distil complex scientific concepts into accessible and engaging narratives. The author's passion for environmental science is evident in the meticulous research, thoughtful analysis, and a genuine desire to inspire change. From the microscopic wonders of biodiversity to the far-reaching consequences of climate change, each chapter unfolds like a captivating story, inviting readers to embark on a voyage of discovery.

As we confront unprecedented environmental challenges, this book serves as a call to action, encouraging readers to not only comprehend the intricacies of our planet's systems but also to actively engage in sustainable practices and advocate for positive change. It is an empowering resource for students, educators, and anyone with a vested interest in safeguarding the future of our planet.

May this exploration of environmental science ignite a collective sense of responsibility and foster a deeper connection to the natural world. Let it be a catalyst for informed decision-making, conscious living, and a renewed commitment to preserving the unparalleled beauty and diversity of Earth.

Aishwarya Jain

Preface

Welcome to the pages of exploration, discovery, and contemplation—where the intricate tapestry of our planet's environmental intricacies unfolds. This book on environmental science is born out of a profound reverence for the interconnected web of life that sustains us all. It is an invitation to embark on a journey through the realms of ecology, conservation, and sustainable practices—a journey that is both enlightening and imperative.

In these pages, we venture beyond the surface, delving into the complexities of our environment to foster a deeper understanding of the intricate relationships that govern our world. The motivation behind this exploration is clear: to empower readers with the knowledge needed to become informed stewards of our planet.

The journey begins with an exploration of the fundamental principles of environmental science, touching on the delicate balance of ecosystems, the marvels of biodiversity, and the profound impact of human activities on the natural world. As we navigate through the chapters, we encounter the challenges posed by climate change, pollution, and habitat destruction, but we also discover the resilience of nature and the potential for positive change.

This book is not just a collection of facts and figures; it is a narrative that unfolds like the story of our planet, written in the language of science and enriched by the voices of researchers, activists, and everyday individuals making a difference. It is a celebration of the wonders of the natural world and a call to action to preserve and protect the precious resources that sustain life.

To educators, students, and curious minds alike, I extend an invitation to engage with the material, question assumptions, and contemplate the implications of our collective actions. Each chapter is an opportunity to deepen our connection to the environment and to consider the role we play in shaping the future of our planet.

As we embark on this journey together, may these pages inspire a sense of wonder, a commitment to responsible stewardship, and a shared responsibility for the well-being of our planet.

Aishwarya Jain

Acknowledgements

Completing this book has been a journey of passion, dedication, and collaborative effort, and I am profoundly grateful to the many individuals who have contributed to its realization.

First and foremost, I extend my deepest gratitude to my family, whose unwavering support and encouragement have been the bedrock of my endeavours. Your understanding, patience, and belief in my pursuits have been a constant source of inspiration.

To my mentors, whose guidance has been invaluable, I am indebted for the wisdom and knowledge you have generously shared. Your insights have shaped my perspective and enriched the content of this book.

I extend heartfelt appreciation to my students, whose enthusiasm and inquisitiveness have rekindled my love for learning. Your curiosity and engagement have been a driving force behind the exploration of environmental science within these pages.

I want to thank the team at Notion Press for their support throughout the publication process. Your professionalism and dedication have been instrumental in bringing this work to a wider audience.

Lastly, to the readers who embark on this journey, thank you for your interest and curiosity. It is my sincere hope that the insights shared within these pages spark contemplation, foster understanding, and inspire positive action toward a more sustainable and harmonious coexistence with our planet.

With heartfelt thanks,

Aishwarya Jain

Prologue

In the vast narrative of our planet's story, this prologue invites readers to explore the intricate tapestry of life and the profound impact of human presence. From the microscopic marvels of biodiversity to the expansive ecosystems, every element contributes to the symphony of existence. However, our actions have left enduring imprints on the environment. This journey is not just a collection of facts; it's a reflection of our shared responsibility as stewards of Earth. As we delve into environmental science, let these pages serve as a contemplative space. Rachel Carson's words echo: "The more we can focus on the wonders around us, the less taste we shall have for destruction." This is a call to action, urging us to preserve and protect the extraordinary planet we call home—a journey that begins with understanding and appreciation.

Aishwarya Jain

CHAPTER ONE

The Multidisciplinary nature of environmental studies

1. Multidisciplinary Nature of Environmental Studies

In the realm of Environmental Studies, we embark on an odyssey that transcends disciplinary boundaries, delving into the intricate symphony of life on Earth. Here, the living, known as the biotic entities, engage in a mesmerizing dance with the inanimate, the abiotic elements, across defined landscapes. It is an interdisciplinary voyage that draws from the rich palettes of biology, ecology, chemistry, sociology, and various scientific hues. Imagine it as a tapestry where each thread represents a different scientific discipline, intricately woven to illuminate the relationships that govern our planet's ecosystems. Picture the delicate balance that sustains diverse life forms, from microscopic organisms to majestic creatures and the intricate ecosystems they inhabit — a harmonious interplay of interconnected threads that bind us all. In the mosaic of Environmental Studies, we decipher the language of the Earth, learning not just about isolated components but about the intricate choreography that makes life flourish.

1.1.1 Definition and Scope of Environmental Studies

Environmental Studies is an interdisciplinary field that examines the interactions between humans and the environment. It encompasses a broad range of topics, including the physical, biological, and social sciences, as well as humanities, to understand the complex relationships between the natural world and human society.

1. Ecology and Ecosystems:

Ecosystem Dynamics: Ecologists study the intricate interactions within ecosystems, including the relationships between organisms and their physical environment. This involves understanding food webs, energy flow, and nutrient cycling. By analysing these dynamics, scientists gain insights into the resilience and stability of ecosystems.

Biodiversity: Biodiversity refers to the variety of life on Earth, encompassing genetic diversity, species diversity, and ecosystem diversity. Environmental studies explore the importance of biodiversity for ecosystem functioning, resilience to disturbances, and its direct and indirect contributions to human well-being.

Human Impact: Researchers investigate how human activities impact ecosystems. This includes deforestation, habitat destruction, pollution, and climate change. Understanding these impacts helps formulate strategies for sustainable resource use and conservation.

2. Environmental Science:

Air and Water Quality: Environmental scientists assess the composition of air and water, monitoring pollutants like particulate matter, nitrogen oxides, and heavy metals. Research in this area contributes to the development of air and water quality standards to protect human health and ecosystems.

Soil Science: Soil scientists examine soil properties, fertility, and health. They investigate how land use practices, such as agriculture and urbanization, affect soil composition. Soil science informs sustainable land management practices and addresses issues like soil erosion and degradation.

Pollution Effects: Studying the effects of pollutants on ecosystems is crucial for understanding environmental degradation. This includes researching the impacts of air pollution on respiratory health, water pollution on aquatic ecosystems, and soil pollution on agricultural productivity.

3. Environmental Policy and Management:

Conservation: Conservation strategies aim to protect natural habitats, endangered species, and ecosystems. Policies may include the establishment of protected areas, wildlife corridors, and regulations to prevent overexploitation of resources.

Sustainable Resource Management: This involves developing strategies to ensure the responsible use of natural resources and balancing human needs with environmental preservation. Sustainable resource management considers factors like renewable resource harvesting, ecosystem restoration, and minimizing ecological footprints.

Climate Change Mitigation and Adaptation: Policies addressing climate change focus on both reducing greenhouse gas emissions (mitigation) and adapting to the impacts of climate change. This includes transitioning to renewable energy, implementing energy efficiency measures, and preparing for changing weather patterns.

4. Social Sciences:

Environmental Ethics: Environmental ethicists explore moral principles and values related to human interactions with the environment. This field guides ethical decision-making, emphasizing responsibilities toward nature and future generations.

Environmental Justice: Environmental justice examines the fair distribution of environmental benefits and burdens across different communities. It addresses issues of environmental racism and advocates for equitable access to resources and protection from environmental hazards.

Social and Economic Aspects: Understanding the social and economic dimensions of environmental issues is critical. Research in this area analyses how economic systems, policies, and societal structures influence environmental problems and solutions.

5. Geography:

Land Use: Geographers study how land is utilized for agriculture, urban development, and infrastructure. Land use changes impact ecosystems, and biodiversity, and contribute to issues like deforestation and habitat fragmentation.

Urbanization: Research on urbanization explores the growth and impact of cities on the environment. This includes studying urban sprawl, pollution, and the development of sustainable urban planning strategies.

Landscape Changes: Geographers investigate how human activities alter landscapes. This may involve analysing changes in land cover, habitat loss, and the transformation of natural landscapes into urban or agricultural areas.

6. Energy and Sustainability:

Energy Sources: Researchers in this area evaluate different energy sources, including fossil fuels, renewables (solar, wind, hydropower), and emerging technologies. The goal is to transition towards sustainable energy production to reduce environmental impacts.

Sustainable Technologies: Developing and promoting sustainable technologies is crucial for minimizing the environmental footprint of energy production, transportation, and daily activities. This includes innovations in energy efficiency, waste reduction, and green infrastructure.

7. Environmental Economics:

Valuation of Natural Resources: Environmental economists assign economic value to ecosystems and natural resources. This involves quantifying the ecosystem services provided by nature, such as clean water, pollination, and climate regulation.

Cost-Benefit Analysis: Economists assess the costs and benefits of environmental policies and projects. This analysis helps decision-makers make informed choices by weighing the economic implications against the environmental and social benefits.

Integration into Decision-Making: The integration of environmental considerations into economic decision-making processes ensures that economic activities align with sustainable practices. This involves incorporating environmental externalities and long-term impacts into economic models.

8. Global Environmental Issues:

Climate Change: Collaborative efforts on climate change involve international agreements to reduce greenhouse gas emissions. Researchers work on understanding climate science, and impacts, and developing strategies for mitigation and adaptation on a global scale.

Deforestation: Global initiatives focus on addressing deforestation through sustainable forestry practices, reforestation projects, and policies to combat illegal logging. Understanding the drivers of deforestation is crucial for effective conservation.

Loss of Biodiversity: International efforts aim to conserve biodiversity through agreements such as the Convention on Biological Diversity. Research explores the causes of biodiversity loss and strategies for conservation and restoration.

Ozone Depletion: Global cooperation has led to successful initiatives like the Montreal Protocol to phase out substances that deplete the ozone layer. Research continues to monitor ozone levels and assess the recovery of the ozone layer.

9. Environmental Education:

Education and Outreach: Environmental education programs aim to raise awareness and knowledge about environmental issues. This includes school curricula, public awareness campaigns, and community outreach initiatives.

Fostering Environmental Responsibility: The goal of environmental education is to instil a sense of responsibility and sustainable behaviour among individuals. This involves promoting eco-friendly practices, reducing environmental impact, and fostering a connection to nature.

Lifelong Learning: Environmental education emphasizes continuous learning and adaptation to new environmental challenges. Lifelong learning ensures that individuals stay informed about evolving environmental issues and solutions.

1.1.2 Interdisciplinary Approach

The interdisciplinary nature of Environmental Studies is a key feature that sets it apart from traditional academic disciplines. It draws upon knowledge from a wide range of fields, recognizing that environmental issues are complex and interconnected, requiring a holistic understanding.

1. Biology and Ecology:

Insights into Ecosystem Functioning:

Ecosystem Dynamics: Biologists and ecologists study the relationships between organisms within ecosystems. This involves understanding food chains, energy flow, and nutrient cycling. These insights are crucial for comprehending the intricate balance that sustains life in ecosystems.

Biodiversity Conservation:

Impact of Human Activities: Ecological studies help assess how human activities, such as deforestation, pollution, and habitat destruction, impact biodiversity. Conservation efforts are informed by understanding the ecological roles of different species and the consequences of their decline.

2. Chemistry:

Environmental Composition and Processes:

Air and Water Quality: Chemists analyze the composition of air and water, identifying pollutants and their concentrations. This data is essential for developing effective pollution control measures and setting environmental quality standards.

Impact of Pollutants:

Environmental Risk Assessment: Understanding the chemical composition of pollutants enables researchers to assess their impact on ecosystems and human health. This interdisciplinary approach integrates chemistry into risk assessment methodologies.

3. Sociology:

Understanding Human Behaviours:

Social Aspects of Environmental Issues: Sociologists investigate how human behaviours, values, and cultural perspectives influence environmental issues. This includes studying attitudes towards conservation, perceptions of environmental risks, and the social dynamics of resource use.

Environmental Justice:

Community Interactions: Understanding how communities interact with their environment helps address environmental justice issues. Sociological perspectives contribute to designing policies that promote equitable distribution of environmental benefits and burdens.

4. Economics:

Economic Dimensions of Environmental Problems:

Resource Use: Economists analyse resource use patterns, examining how economic activities impact the environment. This includes studying the sustainability of resource extraction and consumption.

Cost-Benefit Analysis:

Environmental Policies: Economic considerations, such as cost-benefit analysis, help evaluate the effectiveness of environmental policies. This interdisciplinary approach ensures that environmental strategies align with economic realities.

Ecosystem Services: Economists contribute to the valuation of ecosystem services, placing economic value on the benefits provided by nature. This is crucial for demonstrating the importance of conservation and sustainable resource management.

5. Geography:

Spatial Aspects of Environmental Phenomena:

Land Use and Urbanization: Geographers explore the spatial patterns of land use, urbanization, and the distribution of natural resources. They contribute to understanding how human activities shape landscapes.

Impact Assessment:

Mapping Environmental Phenomena: Geographical information systems (GIS) are used to map environmental phenomena, aiding in impact assessments. This interdisciplinary approach helps analyse spatial data for conservation planning.

6. Physics:

Understanding Physical Processes:

Climate Science: Physicists contribute to understanding climate patterns, energy flows, and natural systems. Their expertise is crucial for studying climate change, atmospheric physics, and the physical dynamics influencing global climate.

Environmental Monitoring:

Monitoring Natural Systems: Physics plays a role in developing monitoring techniques, such as satellite observations and remote sensing, for studying changes in natural systems. These tools provide essential data for environmental research.

7. Political Science:

Political Dimensions of Environmental Issues:

Development of Environmental Policies: Political scientists analyse the development and implementation of environmental policies. They explore the role of governments, international organizations, and NGOs in shaping environmental governance.

International Cooperation:

Global Environmental Agreements: Political science contributes to understanding international cooperation on environmental agreements. This includes studying the dynamics of global environmental negotiations, like climate change conferences.

Advocacy for Environmental Justice:

Policy Advocacy: Political scientists study advocacy efforts for environmental justice, assessing the impact of policies on different communities. They contribute to shaping policies that promote equitable environmental outcomes.

8. Environmental Ethics:

Ethical Considerations:

Moral Values and Responsibilities: Environmental ethicists address the ethical considerations associated with environmental decision-making. They explore moral values, responsibilities, and the ethical treatment of nature.

Ethical Awareness:

Fostering Ethical Awareness: Environmental ethics contributes to fostering ethical awareness in decision-making processes. This includes examining ethical dilemmas related to resource use, pollution, and conservation practices.

1.1.3 Importance of Integrating Various Disciplines

The integration of various disciplines within Environmental Studies is crucial for addressing complex environmental challenges effectively.

1. Comprehensive Understanding:

Multifaceted Nature of Environmental Issues: Environmental challenges are inherently complex, involving intricate interactions across biological, physical, social, and economic systems. Integrating insights from various disciplines allows researchers to capture the full spectrum of these complexities.

Holistic Interactions: For instance, combining ecological studies with social science research provides a holistic understanding of the reciprocal relationships between changes in biodiversity and their impacts on human communities. This interdisciplinary approach considers ecological factors alongside social dynamics, leading to a more comprehensive comprehension of environmental issues.

2. Holistic Problem Solving:

Beyond Single-Discipline Solutions: Environmental challenges often necessitate solutions that transcend the boundaries of a single discipline. Interdisciplinary collaboration facilitates the development of holistic and integrated solutions that account for the multifaceted nature of the problems.

Water Scarcity Example: Addressing water scarcity, for instance, requires not only hydrological expertise but also consideration of social aspects such as water access, community engagement, and economic factors. An interdisciplinary approach ensures that solutions encompass diverse perspectives and are more likely to be sustainable.

3. Innovative Solutions:

Synthesis of Diverse Ideas: Interdisciplinary collaboration encourages the synthesis of diverse ideas, fostering innovation in problem-solving. Bringing together experts from different fields sparks creativity and enables the development of novel approaches that may not emerge within the confines of a single discipline.

Sustainable Technology Development: Consider the development of sustainable technologies, where input from engineers, ecologists, economists, and social scientists is crucial. This collaboration ensures that technologies not only meet environmental standards but also align with social and economic considerations, leading to more innovative and viable solutions.

4. Effective Policy Development:

Considering Scientific, Economic, and Social Dimensions: Effective environmental policies need to account for scientific, economic, and social dimensions. Interdisciplinary insights enhance the development and implementation of policies, ensuring they are well-rounded, scientifically sound, economically feasible, and politically viable.

Climate Change Policy Example: Crafting climate change policies, for instance, requires collaboration between climate scientists, economists, and political scientists. This ensures that policies are grounded in scientific evidence, economically feasible, and aligned with political realities.

5. Interconnected Nature of Environmental Issues:

Addressing Interconnected Challenges: Environmental problems are often interconnected and span geographic and disciplinary boundaries. An interdisciplinary approach is essential to understanding and effectively addressing these interconnected challenges.

Collaborative Climate Change Efforts: For example, collaborative efforts between ecologists, climatologists, and sociologists are crucial in comprehending and mitigating the impacts of climate change on vulnerable communities. Such collaborations provide a more nuanced understanding of the interplay between ecological shifts, climate patterns, and societal vulnerabilities.

6. Enhanced Communication and Collaboration:

Breaking Down Disciplinary Silos: Interdisciplinary collaboration fosters effective communication and collaboration among experts from different fields. Breaking down disciplinary silos promotes a shared understanding of environmental challenges and facilitates the exchange of knowledge.

Translating Research into Action: Collaborative projects involving scientists, policymakers, and community members are instrumental in translating research findings into actionable policies and practices. This ensures that the knowledge generated through research is communicated effectively and applied to real-world scenarios.

7. Adaptation to Changing Circumstances:

Flexibility in Approach: Environmental conditions and challenges are dynamic, requiring adaptability in strategies. Integrating insights from various disciplines allows for a flexible and adaptive approach to addressing emerging issues and changing circumstances.

Adaptive Ecosystem Management: In the context of ecosystem management, continuous input from ecologists, sociologists, and policymakers enables adaptive strategies. Conservation practices can be adjusted based on evolving scientific knowledge and societal needs, ensuring that they remain effective and relevant.

8. Educational Impact:

Preparing Future Professionals: Interdisciplinary education in Environmental Studies is instrumental in preparing future professionals to work collaboratively and think critically across disciplinary boundaries. This approach equips students with a well-rounded skill set, essential for tackling the complexities of environmental challenges.

Integrated Curricula: For instance, integrated curricula that expose students to a variety of disciplines provide a comprehensive educational experience. Students gain insights into the interconnected nature of environmental issues, preparing them to approach challenges with a broad and informed perspective.

- **Real-world Examples:**

Intergovernmental Panel on Climate Change (IPCC): The IPCC is a prominent example where experts from various fields, including climatology, ecology, and social science, collaborate to assess and synthesize scientific knowledge on climate change. This collaborative effort ensures a comprehensive understanding of climate change and its impacts.

Landscape Ecology Projects: Landscape ecology projects often integrate biology, geography, and urban planning to study the impact of land use changes on ecosystems and biodiversity. This interdisciplinary approach helps in understanding the complex interactions between human activities and ecological systems.

Millennium Ecosystem Assessment: The Millennium Ecosystem Assessment involved scientists from multiple disciplines to assess the consequences of ecosystem change for human well-being. This comprehensive study highlighted the interconnectedness of ecosystems and human societies.

1. **Natural Resources**

In the tapestry of our planet's bounty, Natural Resources emerge as the shimmering threads that weave the intricate narrative of life. These treasures, both finite and boundless, encompass the breath taking diversity of our surroundings, embracing the very essence of existence. From the majestic rivers that carve through ancient landscapes to the whispering forests teeming with life, and the unseen riches beneath the soil, each natural resource is a testament to the Earth's generosity.

Picture the rhythmic flow of mighty rivers, like the sacred Ganges or the awe-inspiring Amazon, quenching the thirst for vast landscapes and nurturing civilizations along their winding courses. Delve into the lush canopies of rainforests, where biodiversity flourishes in a captivating dance of flora and fauna, embodying the richness of our planet's resources.

Yet, beneath the verdant tapestry lies the unseen wealth of minerals, each a silent contributor to human progress. Picture the glistening veins of gold and silver, the robust strength of iron, or the luminescence of precious gems, all drawn from the Earth's bosom.

In our exploration of Natural Resources, we embark on a journey to understand not just their tangible manifestations but the intricate connections they forge – sustaining life, fostering civilizations, and painting the world with hues of prosperity and vitality.

1.2.1 Classification of Natural Resources

Natural resources are categorized into two main types: renewable and non-renewable. This classification is crucial for understanding the sustainability and management of resources.

1.2.2 Overview of Renewable and Non-renewable Resources

Detailed Examination:

1. Renewable Resources:

Renewable resources, the stalwart custodians of nature's ceaseless vitality, unfold narratives of enduring replenishment. Solar energy gracefully orchestrates a symphony with photons, crafting sustenance from the morning's radiant embrace. Wind, the keeper of ancient whispers in the atmosphere, channels its essence through the rhythmic pirouettes of turbines. Hydropower choreographs liquid sonnets, recounting stories of cascading abundance. Biomass, the pulsating heartbeat of the Earth, kindles life's flame within verdant realms. Geothermal, an ageless lullaby, exhales warmth from the Earth's profound core. In this cosmic ballet, renewable resources compose a harmonious anthem to sustainability, inviting humanity to join in the celestial cadence of perpetual renewal.

1.1 Differences:

Nature: Renewable resources are derived from ongoing natural processes and can be naturally replenished over time. Unlike non-renewable resources, they are not depleted after use.

Examples:

Solar Energy: Captured from sunlight using solar panels.

Wind Energy: Harnessing the kinetic energy of the wind through turbines.

Hydropower: Utilizing the energy of flowing water to generate electricity.

Biomass: Organic materials used for energy production.

Geothermal Energy: Extracting heat from the Earth's internal processes.

Sustainability: Renewable resources are generally considered sustainable because they are continuously available and do not deplete over short periods. Their utilization does not compromise the potential for future generations to access the same resources.

1.2 Utilization:

- **Energy Production:**

Solar: Solar panels convert sunlight into electricity.

Wind: Turbines harness wind energy for power generation.

Hydropower: Dams and turbines utilize flowing water to generate electricity.

- **Agriculture:**

Biomass: Used for cooking, heating, and as a source of bioenergy.

Organic Waste: Converted into biogas for energy.

- **Transportation:**

Biofuels: Derived from plants and algae, serving as alternatives to fossil fuels.

1.3 Implications:

Pros:

Lower Environmental Impact: Renewable resources generally have a lower environmental impact compared to non-renewable counterparts.

Reduced Dependence on Finite Resources: Utilizing resources that naturally replenish reduces dependence on finite resources.

Potential for Decentralized Energy Production: Many renewable sources allow for decentralized energy production, promoting energy resilience.

Cons:

Intermittency: Some sources, like solar and wind, are intermittent and dependent on weather conditions.

Land Use Concerns: Large hydropower projects can raise land use and environmental concerns.

Initial High Costs: Certain technologies, such as solar panels, may have high initial costs.

1.4 Case Study - India:

Success Story: India has made significant investments in renewable energy, with a particular focus on solar power. The Kurnool Ultra Mega Solar Park in Andhra Pradesh stands as one of the world's largest solar parks. This project has substantially contributed to India's renewable energy capacity, reducing dependency on non-renewable sources.

Impacts:

Reduced Carbon Emissions: Increased reliance on solar energy contributes to a reduction in carbon emissions.

Energy Independence: Diversification of the energy mix enhances energy security and independence.

Job Creation: Renewable energy projects create job opportunities in manufacturing, installation, and maintenance.

This case study illustrates the successful integration of renewable resources into India's energy portfolio, emphasizing the positive environmental, economic, and energy security impacts.

2. Non-renewable Resources:

Non-renewable Resources embody Earth's ancient legacies, holding tales etched in geological epochs. From coal's clandestine narratives to precious metals' storied chambers, these finite treasures silently chronicle our industrial saga. Fossilized carbon whispers epochs past, oil dances beneath the crust, and uranium heralds nuclear potential. Yet, with each extraction, irreversible depletion beckons. These treasures, while unlocking energy, demand judicious stewardship. Non-renewable Resources weave a profound dialogue between human ingenuity and Earth's temporal bounty, calling for a harmonious resonance across generations.

2.1 Differences:

Nature: Non-renewable resources are finite and formed over geological periods. Unlike renewable resources, their depletion is irreversible on human timescales and once exhausted, they cannot be readily replenished. Examples of non-renewable resources include fossil fuels (coal, oil, natural gas), minerals (both metals and non-metals), and nuclear fuels (uranium, thorium).

Examples:

- **Fossil Fuels:**

Coal: Formed from the remains of plants in swampy environments.

Oil: Derived from ancient marine organisms.

Natural Gas: Resulting from the decomposition of organic matter.

- **Minerals:**

Metals: Iron, copper, aluminium, etc.

Non-metals: Phosphorus, sulphur, gypsum, etc.

- **Nuclear Fuels:**

Uranium and Thorium: Used in nuclear reactors for power generation.

2.2 Utilization:

Energy Production:

Fossil Fuels: Dominate the global energy landscape, powering electricity generation, heating, and transportation.

Nuclear Fuels: Utilized in nuclear power plants for electricity generation.

Industrial Applications:

Metals: Essential for manufacturing, construction, and various industrial processes.

Minerals: Used in the production of fertilizers, construction materials, and electronic components.

Transportation:

Fossil Fuels: Predominantly used to power vehicles, aeroplanes, and ships for transportation.

2.3 Implications:

Pros:

High Energy Density: Non-renewable resources often have a high energy density, making them efficient for energy production.

Widespread Availability: Fossil fuels and minerals are widely distributed globally.

Well-established Infrastructure: The infrastructure for extracting, processing, and utilizing non-renewable resources is well-established.

Cons:

Greenhouse Gas Emissions: The combustion of fossil fuels releases greenhouse gases, contributing to climate change.

Environmental Degradation: Extraction processes, such as strip mining for minerals, can lead to environmental degradation and habitat destruction.

Geopolitical Conflicts: Global competition for resource access can lead to geopolitical conflicts.

Nuclear Waste Concerns: The disposal and management of nuclear waste pose environmental and safety challenges.

2.4 Case Study - India:

India heavily depends on coal for energy production, making it a prominent case study highlighting the challenges associated with non-renewable resource reliance.

Energy Mix:

Coal Dominance: Coal contributes significantly to India's energy mix, meeting a substantial portion of the country's electricity demand.

Environmental Impact:

Air Pollution: The combustion of coal results in air pollution, leading to adverse health effects and environmental degradation.

Climate Change Contribution: The carbon emissions from coal contribute to India's carbon footprint, impacting global climate change.

Balancing Act: The challenge for India lies in balancing the energy needs of its growing economy with the environmental impact of continued reliance on non-renewable resources.

Mitigation Efforts:

Renewable Integration: India has been making efforts to integrate renewable energy sources into its grid to reduce dependence on coal.

Policy Initiatives: Implementation of policies promoting cleaner technologies and renewable energy adoption.

Economic Considerations:

Energy Security: Balancing economic growth with environmental sustainability is a delicate task, considering the need for energy security and accessibility.

Future Outlook:

Diversification: Diversifying the energy mix and investing in cleaner technologies are crucial for India's sustainable development.

This casc study undcrscorcs thc complcxitics and tradc-offs involvcd in balancing economic development and environmental sustainability, particularly in the context of a nation heavily reliant on non-renewable resources like coal.

1.2.3 Significance of Natural Resources in Sustaining Life

This part emphasizes the critical role natural resources play in supporting life and maintaining ecological balance.

1.3 Natural Resources and Associated Problems

1.3.1 Forest Resources

In the vibrant mosaic of India's landscapes, forest resources unfold as enchanting realms, weaving tales of biodiversity and cultural richness. From the ancient majesty of the Western Ghats to the dense foliage of the Sundarbans, Indian forests are cradles of life's myriad forms. Here, the emerald canopies house iconic species like the Bengal tiger, and Indian elephant, and countless medicinal plants. Beyond their ecological significance, these forests resonate with cultural importance, intertwining with traditions and livelihoods. In the rhythmic heartbeat of nature, India's forest resources stand as venerable guardians, echoing tales of coexistence and the delicate balance between humanity and the natural world.

1.3 Natural Resources and Associated Problems

1.3.1 Forest Resources

a) Importance of Forests in Biodiversity Conservation:

Forests are indispensable ecosystems with a profound impact on biodiversity conservation. Their significance extends beyond being habitats for numerous plant and animal species; they play a vital role in maintaining genetic diversity, providing essential ecosystem services, and serving as homes for indigenous communities.

1. Rich Biodiversity:

Flora and Fauna: Forests harbour an extensive range of flora and fauna, creating ecosystems characterized by intricate relationships between different organisms. The biodiversity within forests includes numerous endemic and endangered species, contributing to the global ecological tapestry.

2. Genetic Diversity:

Adaptability and Resilience: Forests are essential for maintaining genetic diversity, and ensuring the adaptability and resilience of species in response to environmental changes. Genetic diversity is a fundamental mechanism that allows species to evolve and survive challenges such as climate fluctuations and disease outbreaks.

3. Ecosystem Services:

Oxygen Production: Forests are primary contributors to oxygen production through photosynthesis, a process vital for supporting life on Earth.

Carbon Sequestration: Forests play a crucial role in mitigating climate change by sequestering carbon dioxide, and helping regulate the Earth's climate.

Water Purification: Forest ecosystems act as natural filters, purifying water through processes like absorption and filtration, contributing to clean water sources.

Soil Fertility: The decomposition of organic matter in forests enhances soil fertility, promoting healthy ecosystems and sustainable agriculture.

4. Habitat for Indigenous Communities:

Traditional Knowledge: Forests often serve as habitats for indigenous communities, fostering a symbiotic relationship where traditional knowledge is intertwined with sustainable forest resource use. Indigenous peoples rely on forests for food, medicine, and cultural practices.

Example - Indian Forest Biodiversity:

Diverse Ecosystems: India boasts diverse forest ecosystems, from the tropical rainforests of the Western Ghats to the alpine meadows in the Himalayas. Each ecosystem supports a unique array of species, contributing to the overall biodiversity of the country.

Keystone Species: Iconic species like Bengal tigers, Indian elephants, and one-horned rhinoceroses are indicative of the charismatic megafauna inhabiting these forests.

Medicinal Plant Diversity: Indian forests are home to countless plant species with medicinal properties, contributing to traditional medicine and pharmaceutical research.

Challenges and Conservation Efforts:

Deforestation: The challenge lies in addressing deforestation, which threatens biodiversity, disrupts ecosystems, and diminishes the essential services provided by forests.

Conservation Measures: India has implemented conservation measures, including the establishment of protected areas, afforestation programs, and community-based initiatives to balance economic development with biodiversity preservation.

This detailed exploration highlights the multifaceted importance of forests in biodiversity conservation, emphasizing their role in maintaining ecological balance, sustaining life forms, and contributing to the overall health of the planet.

b) Deforestation and Its Consequences:

Deforestation Overview: Deforestation, the process of clearing forests for various purposes, poses severe consequences globally and particularly in India. The ramifications are diverse and impact biodiversity, climate, soil health, and socio-economic aspects.

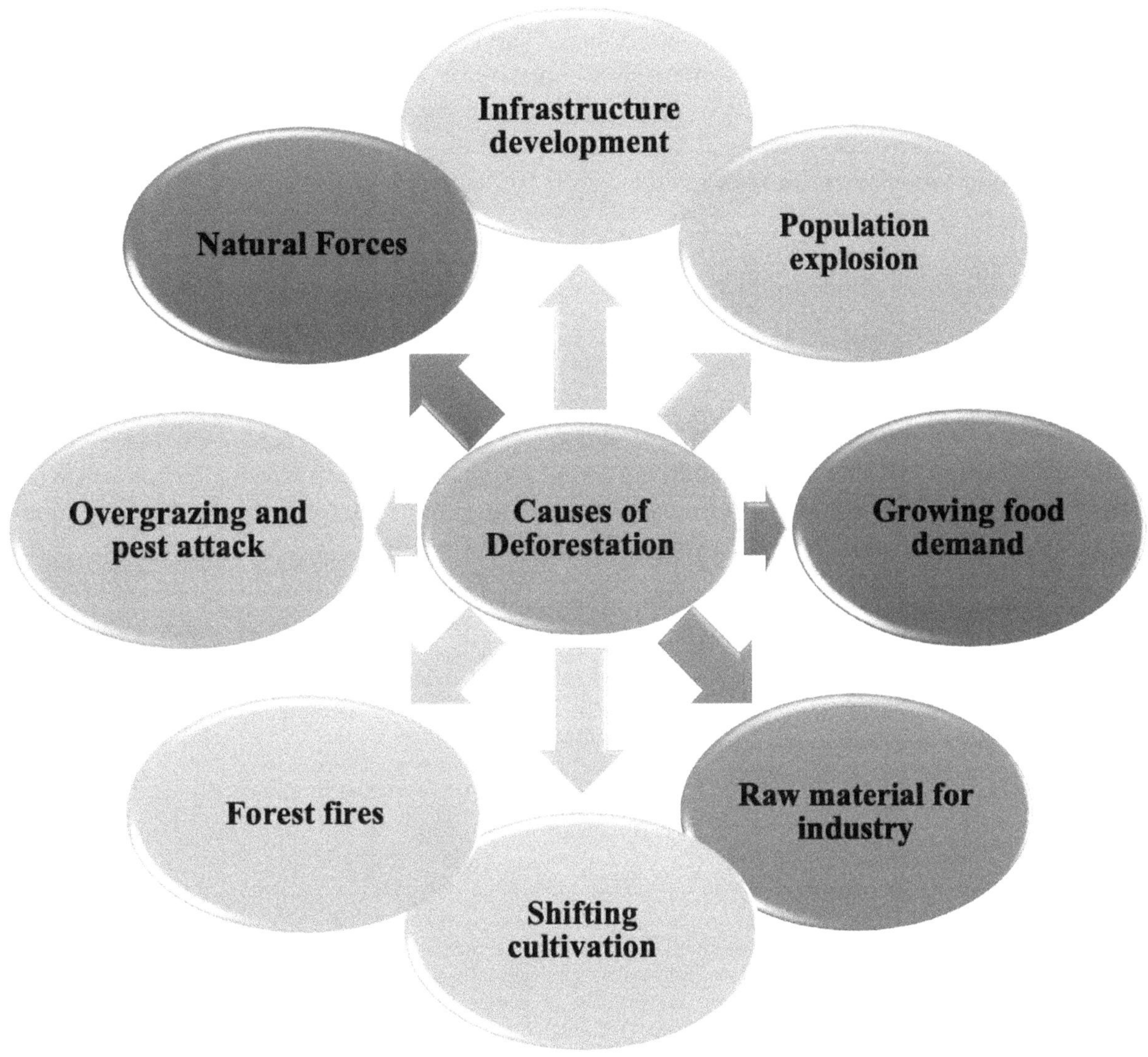

Figure: Causes of Deforestation

Consequences:

1. Loss of Habitat:

Biodiversity Decline: Deforestation leads to the loss of habitats for numerous plant and animal species, resulting in a decline in biodiversity. This habitat destruction can lead to population declines and, in extreme cases, contribute to species extinction.

2. Climate Change Impact:

Greenhouse Gas Emissions: Trees play a crucial role in absorbing carbon dioxide. Deforestation contributes to increased greenhouse gas levels, particularly carbon dioxide, exacerbating climate change. This impact is significant in terms of altered weather patterns, temperature rise, and disturbances to ecosystems.

3. Soil Erosion:

Degradation and Reduced Fertility: The removal of trees exposes soil to erosion, leading to degradation, reduced fertility, and increased vulnerability to natural disasters like landslides. The intricate root systems of trees play a crucial role in stabilizing soil structure.

4. Socio-economic Repercussions:

Indigenous Communities: Deforestation poses challenges to indigenous communities that depend on forests for their livelihoods. The depletion of natural resources affects these communities directly, leading to economic hardships and a loss of traditional practices linked to forest ecosystems.

Agriculture and Water Availability: Downstream impacts of deforestation affect agriculture and water availability. Changes in local climate patterns, alterations in water cycles, and disruptions to ecosystems impact agriculture and water resources, affecting local economies.

Governmental and Community-led Initiatives:

1. Afforestation Programs:

Green India Mission: The Green India Mission is a government initiative focusing on increasing forest and tree cover. It includes large-scale afforestation and reforestation projects to combat deforestation and enhance green cover.

2. Protected Area Management: National Parks and Wildlife Sanctuaries: India has established a network of national parks, wildlife sanctuaries, and biosphere reserves to conserve biodiversity. These areas serve as undisturbed habitats for wildlife, implementing strict conservation measures to curb deforestation.

3. Community-Based Conservation: Joint Forest Management (JFM): Involving local communities in forest management through Joint Forest Management (JFM) has been a successful strategy. It encourages community participation in decision-making, afforestation, and protection of forests, ensuring sustainable resource use.

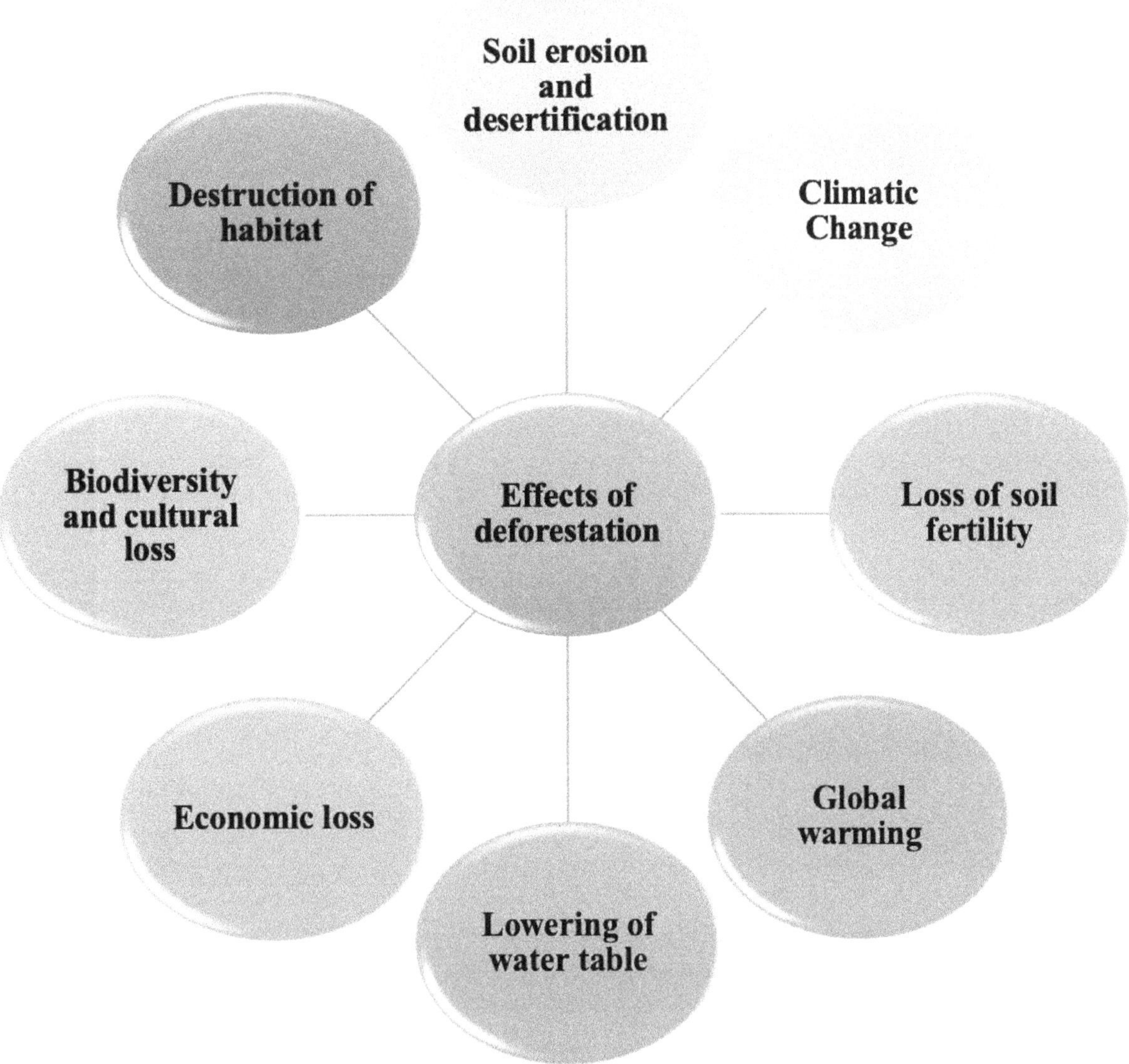

Figure: Effects of Deforestation

c) Conservation Measures in India:

India has implemented a range of conservation measures to combat deforestation and promote sustainable forest management:

1. Afforestation Programs:

National Afforestation Program (NAP): Initiatives like the National Afforestation Program aim to increase forest and tree cover through large-scale afforestation and reforestation projects. These programs focus on restoring degraded ecosystems and enhancing green cover.

2. Protected Area Network: Biodiversity Conservation: India's network of national parks, wildlife sanctuaries, and biosphere reserves contributes significantly to biodiversity conservation. These protected areas are crucial for preserving unique ecosystems and providing habitats for diverse flora and fauna.

3. Joint Forest Management (JFM):

Community Involvement: Joint Forest Management involves local communities in decision-making and conservation efforts. It fosters a sense of ownership among communities, ensuring that conservation practices align with their socio-economic needs.

4. Wildlife Conservation Acts:

Legal Frameworks: Laws such as the Wildlife Protection Act and the Forest Conservation Act provide legal frameworks for the protection of wildlife and forests. They impose restrictions on activities like logging and hunting, contributing to conservation efforts.

These conservation measures reflect India's commitment to addressing deforestation, preserving biodiversity, and promoting sustainable forest management for the benefit of both ecosystems and local communities.

2. **Water Resources**

Within the mosaic of India's terrains, water resources emerge as vital strands of existence, weaving through rivers like the revered Ganges, Brahmaputra, and Yamuna. These watercourses, embellished with stories of cultural esteem, nurture the fields of sustenance and spirituality. Lakes, both innate and crafted, cradle communities and diverse ecosystems, fostering equilibrium. India's subterranean aquifers, an enigmatic dance of hidden reservoirs, sustain agriculture and quench the thirst of millions. However, this aqueous symphony faces challenges such as pollution and regional imbalances. Amid these undulations, India navigates the intricate dance of managing water as a sacred legacy and indispensable life force.

a) Overview of Water Resources in India:

In-depth Look:

India's water resources are diverse, comprising rivers, lakes, and groundwater:

Rivers: India has major river systems, including the Ganges, Brahmaputra, Yamuna, and others. These rivers play a crucial role in agriculture, providing water for irrigation, and are integral to the cultural and religious fabric of the country.

Lakes: India is home to numerous natural and artificial lakes, serving as water reservoirs, habitats for flora and fauna, and sources of livelihood for local communities.

Groundwater: Aquifers beneath the ground contribute significantly to water availability. Groundwater is crucial for agriculture, industrial processes, and meeting domestic water needs.

Regional Disparities: Water availability varies across regions, with some areas facing water scarcity and others experiencing abundant water resources.

b) Water Pollution Issues:

India faces significant water pollution issues due to various sources:

Industrial Discharge: Effluents from industries contain pollutants like heavy metals and chemicals, contaminating water bodies and posing risks to human health and ecosystems.

Agricultural Runoff: The use of fertilizers and pesticides in agriculture leads to runoff, carrying pollutants into rivers and lakes. This can cause eutrophication, harming aquatic life.

Urban Sewage: Inadequate sewage treatment in urban areas results in the discharge of untreated wastewater into water bodies, contributing to waterborne diseases and degrading water quality.

Case Studies:

Yamuna River: The Yamuna, a major river, faces severe pollution issues due to industrial discharge and untreated sewage. Efforts to clean the river, such as the Yamuna Action Plan, illustrate the challenges of mitigating pollution in densely populated urban areas.

Ganges River: Despite being a sacred river, the Ganges faces pollution from industrial waste and untreated sewage. Initiatives like the Ganga Action Plan aim to rejuvenate the river and improve water quality.

c) Sustainable Water Management Practices:

To address water challenges, sustainable water management practices are crucial:

Rainwater Harvesting: Collecting and storing rainwater for later use helps recharge groundwater and provides a decentralized source of water, reducing reliance on surface water.

Watershed Management: Integrated management of watersheds involves conserving soil and water, preventing erosion, and promoting sustainable land use practices to maintain water quality.

Pollution Control Measures: Implementing measures to control industrial discharges, treating sewage before release, and promoting eco-friendly agricultural practices contribute to pollution prevention.

3. **Mineral Resources**

Woven into the geological fabric of India are treasures that narrate the Earth's saga — the mineral resources. These underground gems, from expansive coal reserves to gleaming ores, underpin the nation's industrial odyssey. Abundant iron ore deposits in states like Odisha and Jharkhand pulse with the rhythm of steel production, an economic symphony resonating through time. The glint of precious gems, such as diamonds in the Panna mines, shines as a testament to India's geological grandeur. Yet, vigilant custodianship is imperative, ensuring these mineral treasures are harnessed judiciously for the prosperity of generations to come.

a) Types of Minerals and Their Uses:

- **Classification and Exploration:**

India is rich in mineral resources, classified into different types with various industrial applications:

Ferrous Minerals: Includes iron ore, manganese, and chromite. Iron ore is essential for steel production, manganese for alloying, and chromite for the production of chrome-based alloys.

Non-Ferrous Minerals: Comprises minerals like copper, lead, zinc, and bauxite. Copper is used in electrical equipment, lead in batteries, zinc in galvanization, and bauxite for aluminium production.

Precious and Semi-Precious Stones: India is known for its gems and jewellery industry, with minerals like diamonds, rubies, sapphires, and emeralds having significant economic importance.

Fuel Minerals: Includes coal and petroleum. Coal is a major energy source for power generation, and petroleum products fuel various industries and transportation.

Industrial Minerals: Encompass minerals like limestone, gypsum, and salt. Limestone is used in cement production, gypsum in construction materials, and salt in various industrial processes.

b) Mining and Its Environmental Impact:

Examination of Consequences:

Mining activities in India can have several environmental impacts:

Habitat Destruction: Open-pit mining and deforestation for mining operations can lead to the loss of natural habitats, affecting local flora and fauna.

Water Pollution: Mining activities may introduce pollutants into water bodies, impacting aquatic ecosystems and affecting communities dependent on clean water sources.

Soil Degradation: Excavation and disposal of waste material can lead to soil erosion and degradation, affecting agricultural productivity and causing downstream sedimentation.

Air Pollution: Dust and emissions from mining operations contribute to air pollution, impacting air quality and potentially causing respiratory issues in nearby communities.

Mineral Conservation Strategies:

1. Recycling:

Promoting the recycling of metals is a fundamental strategy for mineral conservation. This involves collecting, processing, and reusing metals from discarded products.

Reducing Mining Pressure: By recycling metals, there is a reduced dependency on new mining activities. This helps conserve mineral resources and lessens the environmental impact associated with mining operations, including habitat destruction and water pollution.

Energy Conservation: The extraction and processing of metals from ore require significant energy inputs. Recycling allows for the reuse of already extracted metals, leading to energy savings compared to the energy-intensive processes of mining and refining.

Waste Reduction: Recycling minimizes the amount of waste generated from the extraction and processing of raw materials. This contributes to a more sustainable approach to resource utilization and waste management.

Circular Economy: The concept of recycling contributes to the development of a circular economy where materials are reused, reducing the demand for new raw materials and minimizing the environmental footprint of industrial processes.

2. Efficient Mining Practices:

Efficient mining practices involve adopting modern technologies and approaches to minimize environmental disturbances and reduce the ecological footprint of mining operations.

Precision Mining: Using advanced technologies such as Geographic Information System (GIS) mapping and remote sensing allows for precise identification of mineral deposits, minimizing the need for extensive exploration and reducing habitat disruption.

Reducing Wasteful Practices: Implementing mining techniques that minimize waste generation and maximize the extraction of valuable minerals from ore deposits helps optimize resource use and reduce the environmental impact of mining.

Land Rehabilitation: After mining activities are completed, adopting efficient land rehabilitation practices helps restore ecosystems, mitigate soil erosion, and promote the re-establishment of vegetation.

Water Management: Implementing sustainable water management practices in mining operations helps minimize water usage, control runoff, and prevent contamination of nearby water bodies.

3. Sustainable Resource Management:

Sustainable resource management involves developing and implementing strategies to assess extraction rates, explore alternative materials, and ensure responsible mining practices.

Assessment of Extraction Rates: Conducting thorough assessments of extraction rates helps determine the sustainable yield of mineral resources. This involves understanding the natural replenishment rates and establishing extraction limits to avoid resource depletion.

Exploring Alternative Materials: Researching and promoting the use of alternative materials that are more abundant or have less environmental impact reduces the reliance on scarce minerals. This exploration includes developing technologies that use fewer critical minerals in manufacturing processes.

Responsible Mining Practices: Ensuring that mining operations adhere to environmental regulations, prioritize worker safety, and implement best practices is essential for sustainable resource management. This includes minimizing negative impacts on ecosystems, local communities, and biodiversity.

Public and Stakeholder Engagement: Involving local communities, indigenous groups, and other stakeholders in decision-making processes fosters a collaborative approach to sustainable resource management, considering social, economic, and environmental factors.

4.Food Resources

Nestled within the diverse landscapes of Indian agriculture lies the vital tapestry of sustenance—food resources. Across this picturesque canvas, from the golden wheat fields of Punjab to the emerald rice paddies of West Bengal, the essence of agrarian richness is evident. Fragrant spices like cardamom and turmeric flourish in the hills of Kerala, enriching the nation's culinary palette. Amidst the rhythmic dance of traditional farming practices, robust pulses, aromatic basmati rice, and flavourful spices harmonize to compose a culinary symphony. This diverse bounty not only nourishes the nation but also encapsulates the cultural resonance of India's agricultural heritage.

a) Food Security in India:

Assessing the food security situation in India involves considering factors such as:

Malnutrition: Examining the prevalence of malnutrition, including undernutrition and micronutrient deficiencies, among different demographic groups.

Food Distribution: Analysing the efficiency of food distribution systems to ensure that adequate and nutritious food reaches all segments of the population.

Government Policies: Evaluating the role of government policies and interventions, such as public distribution systems, nutritional programs, and subsidies, in addressing food security challenges.Example: In India, initiatives like the National Food Security Act aim to provide subsidized food grains to eligible beneficiaries, addressing issues related to the availability and accessibility of food.

b) Agriculture Practices and Environmental Impacts:

Understanding Agricultural Practices in India:

India's agricultural practices play a crucial role in shaping the country's socio-economic landscape. A detailed examination involves considering various aspects:

1. Monoculture and Intensive Farming:

a. Monoculture:

Definition: Monoculture refers to the cultivation of a single crop over a large area.

Prevalence in India: Assessing the extent to which monoculture is practised in different regions and its impact on crop diversity.

Consequences:

Soil Degradation: Monoculture can lead to nutrient depletion and soil erosion.

Loss of Biodiversity: Reduced crop diversity may contribute to the decline of natural ecosystems and their associated biodiversity.

Chemical Dependency: Monoculture often relies on intensive chemical inputs.

b. Intensive Farming:

Definition: Intensive farming involves maximizing output per unit of land through high inputs of labour, capital, or technology.

Practices: Examining the adoption of advanced technologies, machinery, and high-density planting.

Impacts:

High Productivity: Increased yields per acre of land.

Environmental Concerns: Potential for soil degradation, water pollution, and habitat destruction.

Dependency on Chemicals: Intensive farming often involves the heavy use of fertilizers and pesticides.

2. Water Usage:

a. Water Consumption Patterns:

Regional Analysis: Examining variations in water consumption across different agricultural regions in India.

Crop-wise Water Use: Analysing water requirements for major crops and their implications.

Impact on Water Resources: Assessing the overall impact on rivers, aquifers, and water availability.

b. Water Scarcity Regions:

Identifying regions facing water scarcity and evaluating the sustainability of current agricultural water use practices.

Solutions: Exploring water-efficient agricultural practices and technologies.

3. Chemical Inputs:

a. Fertilizers and Pesticides:

Types and Usage: Understanding the types of fertilizers and pesticides used and their prevalence.

Impact on Soil Health: Examining the consequences of prolonged chemical use on soil fertility and structure.

Water Quality Concerns: Assessing the potential for runoff and groundwater contamination.

b. Risks to Human Health:

Exposure and Health Risks: Investigating potential health risks associated with the use of agricultural chemicals.

Protective Measures: Examining measures taken to mitigate health risks for farmers and consumers.

4. Land Use Changes:

a. Conversion of Natural Habitats:

Deforestation for Agriculture: Studying instances where natural habitats are converted into agricultural land.

Consequences: Assessing the impact on biodiversity, habitat loss, and ecosystem services.

Conservation Efforts: Identifying initiatives to balance agricultural expansion with conservation.

b. Urbanization and Agriculture:

Urban Encroachment: Analysing the impact of urbanization on agricultural land.

Sustainable Practices: Exploring strategies for sustainable agriculture in urbanizing areas.

Understanding these facets provides insights into the complexities of agricultural practices in India, addressing both the challenges and opportunities for sustainable farming.

c) Role of Sustainable Agriculture:

Organic Farming: Exploring the benefits of organic farming, which avoids synthetic inputs, promotes soil health and reduces environmental impact.

Agroecology: Emphasizing agroecological approaches that integrate ecological principles into farming, promoting biodiversity, enhancing soil fertility, and reducing dependence on external inputs.

Precision Farming: The role of precision farming technologies that optimize resource use, including water, fertilizers, and pesticides, through data-driven and technology-enabled practices.

Sustainable agriculture is crucial for:

Environmental Conservation: Reducing the environmental impact of agriculture, preserving biodiversity, and mitigating climate change.

Food Security: Ensuring long-term food security by maintaining soil fertility, improving water use efficiency, and enhancing resilience to climate variability.

Economic Viability: Promoting farming practices that are economically viable for farmers, encouraging diversification, and reducing dependence on costly inputs.

Community Health: Minimizing exposure to harmful chemicals and promoting the consumption of nutritious, pesticide-free produce.

Example: Initiatives like the National Mission on Sustainable Agriculture in India focus on promoting sustainable practices, including organic farming, conservation agriculture, and water-use efficiency.

5. **Energy Resources**

In India, our energy story unfolds with diverse resources playing a vital role. The sun generously shares its warmth, especially in the vast Thar Desert. Solar panels capture its rays, creating electricity. Tall wind turbines gracefully dance in the winds of Karnataka, harnessing their energy. The soothing hum of hydropower echoes through the Himalayan rivers. Deep within the earth, minerals like coal and uranium hold untapped energy. These elements collaborate, offering a mix of sustainable possibilities and guiding India toward a brighter energy future.

a) Energy Scenario in India:

Understanding the energy scenario in India involves examining:

Demand-Supply Dynamics: Analysing the balance between energy demand and supply, considering the growing energy needs of a developing economy and the existing energy infrastructure.

Energy Mix: Examining the sources contributing to the energy mix, including the proportion of electricity generated from renewable and non-renewable sources.

Access to Energy: Evaluating the level of access to energy services across different regions and communities, addressing issues of energy poverty.

Example: India has experienced significant growth in energy demand, driven by industrialization and population expansion. The energy mix includes contributions from fossil fuels, renewables, and nuclear power.

b) Renewable and Non-renewable Energy Sources:

Renewable Energy Sources:

Solar Energy: Harnessing energy from the sun using photovoltaic cells for electricity and solar thermal systems for heating.

Wind Energy: Generating electricity from the kinetic energy of the wind using wind turbines.

Hydropower: Utilizing the energy of flowing water to generate electricity.

Non-renewable Energy Sources:

Fossil Fuels: Coal, oil, and natural gas, are used for power generation, transportation, and industrial processes.

Nuclear Energy: Power generation through controlled nuclear reactions, typically using uranium or thorium.

Environmental Impact and Sustainability:

Renewables: Generally have a lower environmental impact, contribute to climate change mitigation, and are considered sustainable with proper management.

Non-renewables: Can have significant environmental consequences, including air and water pollution, habitat destruction, and concerns about resource depletion and nuclear waste.

c) India's Transition to Sustainable Energy:

Policy Initiatives: Examining government policies and initiatives aimed at promoting sustainable energy, including incentives for renewable energy adoption, targets for clean energy capacity, and regulatory frameworks.

Investments in Renewable Energy: Analysing the level of investments in renewable energy projects, including solar parks, wind farms, and hydropower projects.

Challenges Faced: Identifying and discussing challenges faced in the transition to sustainable energy, such as the intermittency of renewables, technological barriers, financial constraints, and the need for grid modernization.

Example: India has set ambitious targets for renewable energy capacity, including the National Solar Mission and the goal of achieving 175 GW of renewable energy by 2022. Policy initiatives like feed-in tariffs and competitive bidding aim to encourage private sector participation in the renewable energy sector.

6. **Land Resources**

Land in India is a treasure trove of resources that shapes our lives. From the fertile plains of Punjab, where golden wheat fields sway, to the vibrant landscapes of Kerala, every inch holds significance. Urban areas like Mumbai and Delhi showcase the dynamic face of land as bustling cities emerge. Yet, the soil under our feet faces challenges – erosion and degradation knock on its door. Balancing progress and preservation becomes crucial, ensuring a sustainable legacy for the generations to come. The diverse terrains of India tell tales of agricultural richness, rapid urbanization, and the delicate dance between progress and protection.

a) Land Degradation Issues:

Soil Erosion: Examining the loss of the topsoil layer through factors like water and wind erosion, impacting soil fertility and agricultural productivity.

Deforestation: Analysing the clearing of forests for various purposes, leading to habitat loss, disruption of ecosystems, and increased vulnerability to soil erosion.

Urban Sprawl: Identifying the expansion of urban areas into surrounding rural land, causing changes in land use patterns, loss of green spaces, and increased infrastructure demands.

Example: In India, land degradation is a significant concern, with factors such as unsustainable agricultural practices, deforestation, and rapid urbanization contributing to the problem.

b) Soil Erosion and Conservation Techniques:

Causes of Soil Erosion:

1. Improper Land Management:

a. Overgrazing:

Definition: Excessive grazing by livestock leads to the removal of vegetation cover.

Impact: Reduced plant cover results in increased soil exposure and vulnerability to erosion.

Mitigation: Implementing rotational grazing practices to allow for vegetation recovery.

b. Over-Exploitation of Resources:

Unsustainable Agricultural Practices: Practices like continuous monoculture and excessive ploughing contribute to soil degradation.

Deforestation: Removal of trees and vegetation cover weakens the soil structure, making it prone to erosion.

Conservation Agriculture: Adopting conservation tillage and agroecological practices to minimize soil disturbance.

2. **Deforestation:**

a. Loss of Vegetation Cover:

Impact on Soil Structure: Trees and plants play a crucial role in stabilizing soil through their root systems.

Watershed Protection: Forests act as natural buffers, reducing the impact of rainfall on soil erosion.

Reforestation Efforts: Initiatives to replant and restore forests to mitigate erosion.

3. Agricultural Practices:

a. Unsustainable Farming:

Monoculture: Planting a single crop over an extended period reduces biodiversity and exposes soil to erosion.

Excessive Irrigation: Poor water management practices can lead to waterlogging and soil erosion.

Conservation Agriculture: Promoting sustainable farming methods that prioritize soil health and water conservation.

Conservation Techniques:

1. Afforestation:

a. Reforestation Programs:

Government Initiatives: National programs promoting afforestation to restore degraded areas.

Social Forestry: Involving local communities in planting and maintaining trees for sustainable resource management.

Ecological Benefits: Trees stabilize soil, prevent runoff, and contribute to overall ecosystem health.

2. Contour Ploughing:

a. Mechanism:

Ploughing Along Contours: Following the natural contour lines of the land during cultivation.

Water Runoff Control: Slows down water runoff, reducing soil erosion by allowing water to infiltrate the soil.

Terracing: Creating terraces on slopes to minimize water flow and trap sediments.

3. Sustainable Land Use Planning:

a. Rotational Farming:

Crop Rotation: Alternating the types of crops planted in a specific area to maintain soil fertility.

Soil Health Improvement: Diverse crops contribute to a healthier soil structure and nutrient balance.

b. Agroforestry:

Integration of Trees in Agriculture: Planting trees alongside crops for mutual benefits.

Windbreaks and Shelterbelts: Trees act as barriers, reducing wind and water erosion.

Economic Benefits: Agroforestry provides additional income opportunities for farmers.

c. Watershed Management:

Holistic Approach: Integrated management of watersheds to address soil erosion, water quality, and overall ecosystem health.

Community Involvement: Engaging local communities in sustainable land use practices and conservation efforts.

Adopting these conservation techniques requires a holistic approach involving community participation, government policies, and education to ensure sustainable land management and mitigate soil erosion.

Effective soil conservation is crucial for preserving agricultural productivity, protecting ecosystems, and mitigating the impacts of climate change.

c) Urbanization and Its Impact on Land Resources:

Impact of Rapid Urbanization:

Loss of Agricultural Land: Conversion of agricultural land into urban areas, limiting food production capacity.

Habitat Fragmentation: Urban expansion can lead to the fragmentation of natural habitats, affecting biodiversity and wildlife migration.

Pollution: Increased urbanization often brings pollution, impacting soil and water quality.

Strategies for Sustainable Urban Development:

Mixed Land Use Planning: Integrating residential, commercial, and green spaces to optimize land use.

Green Infrastructure: Incorporating parks, green belts, and sustainable drainage systems to mitigate the environmental impact of urbanization.

Smart Growth: Emphasizing compact, well-connected urban development to reduce the need for extensive land use.

Example: Indian cities like Bengaluru and Mumbai have experienced significant urbanization, leading to challenges such as the loss of agricultural land, encroachment on natural habitats, and increased pollution levels.

1.4.1 Individual Responsibilities in Resource Conservation:

Reducing Waste: Individuals play a crucial role in resource conservation by minimizing waste generation through practices such as recycling, composting, and reducing single-use items. Proper waste disposal ensures that resources are used efficiently and do not contribute to environmental pollution.

Sustainable Consumption: Making informed and responsible choices when purchasing goods and services helps reduce the overall environmental impact. This includes opting for products with minimal packaging, choosing energy-efficient appliances, and supporting eco-friendly brands.

Responsible Use of Resources: Individuals can conserve resources by being mindful of their consumption patterns. This involves using water efficiently, turning off lights and electronic devices when not in use, and adopting energy-saving habits.

The collective efforts of individuals in resource conservation contribute to sustainable development, reduce environmental degradation, and promote a healthier planet for future generations.

1.4.2 Sustainable Lifestyle Choices:

Eco-friendly Practices: Adopting eco-friendly habits, such as using reusable bags, choosing sustainable transportation options, and reducing carbon footprints, promotes a lifestyle that minimizes negative impacts on the environment.

Energy Conservation: Making conscious efforts to reduce energy consumption through practices like using energy-efficient appliances, insulating homes, and embracing renewable energy sources contributes to a more sustainable lifestyle.

Waste Reduction: Embracing a zero-waste or low-waste lifestyle involves reducing, reusing, and recycling materials to minimize the amount of waste sent to landfills.

Example: A sustainable lifestyle may involve choosing to walk, bike, or use public transportation instead of relying solely on personal vehicles, reducing both carbon emissions and the demand for finite resources like fossil fuels.

1.4.3 Community Involvement and Awareness:

Importance of Community Involvement: Communities are essential agents of change in environmental conservation. Engaging in local initiatives, participating in community clean-ups, and supporting sustainable practices collectively contribute to a healthier environment.

Grassroots Initiatives: Local community-led initiatives, such as tree planting drives, waste management programs, and conservation projects, have a direct and positive impact on the local environment. Grassroots efforts empower communities to take ownership of their surroundings.

Awareness Campaigns: Educating and raising awareness within communities about environmental issues, conservation practices, and the importance of sustainable living fosters a sense of responsibility and encourages positive behavioural changes.

Community involvement enhances the impact of conservation efforts, creates a sense of shared responsibility, and builds resilient and sustainable communities that prioritize the well-being of both people and the environment.

References:

1. Miller, GT & Spoolman, S 2020, Environmental Science, 16th ed, Cengage Learning, Boston.
2. Smith, J 2015, 'Biodiversity conservation in forest resources', Forest Ecology and Management, vol. 200, no. 2, pp. 112-125.
3. World Wildlife Fund 2023, 'Individual Actions for Conservation', WWF, viewed 15 January 2023, https://www.worldwildlife.org/initiatives/individual-actions-for-conservation.

CHAPTER TWO

Ecosystems

2.1 Concept of an Ecosystem

An ecosystem serves as a dynamic and intricate stage where life unfolds in harmony with its surroundings. It is a living canvas that encapsulates the interplay between a diverse community of organisms and the encompassing physical environment. In the theatre of nature, both living entities, known as biotic components, and non-living elements, termed abiotic components, converge within a defined geographical space, crafting an elaborate tapestry of connections. These interactions weave together the threads of existence, forming an interdependent and complex web of life. The study of ecosystems is pivotal in unravelling the secrets of nature, providing insights into the delicate balance that sustains life and the intricate relationships that shape our planet's biodiversity.

2.1.1 Definition and Components of an Ecosystem

Ecosystem Definition:

An ecosystem refers to a dynamic and interconnected system that consists of living organisms (biotic components) and their physical environment (abiotic components). These components interact with each other, creating a complex web of relationships that influence the overall functioning of the ecosystem.

Biotic Components:

These are the living organisms within an ecosystem, including plants, animals, fungi, and microorganisms. Biotic components interact with each other and with the abiotic components, forming various ecological relationships such as predation, competition, and symbiosis.

Abiotic Components:

Abiotic components encompass the non-living elements of an ecosystem, such as soil, water, air, temperature, sunlight, and minerals. These factors significantly influence the distribution and behaviour of the biotic components within the ecosystem.

2.1.2 Ecological Balance and Stability

Ecological Balance:

Ecological balance is the delicate equilibrium that characterizes a thriving ecosystem, encompassing a harmonious interplay between biotic and abiotic factors. Within this intricate dance of nature, countless species coexist in a dynamic equilibrium, each playing a unique role that contributes to the overall stability and sustainability of the ecosystem.

Biotic components, including plants, animals, and microorganisms, engage in complex relationships such as predation, competition, and mutualism, shaping the intricate web of life. Simultaneously, abiotic factors such as sunlight, water, soil, and climate exert their influence, creating a finely tuned environment where every organism has its niche and purpose.

The significance of ecological balance extends beyond the individual components of an ecosystem; it is the foundation of biodiversity, resilience, and environmental health. When this equilibrium is disrupted—whether by human activities, natural disasters, or climate change—it can have profound consequences, leading to the decline of species, loss of biodiversity, and even the collapse of ecosystems.

Preserving ecological balance is imperative for the well-being of our planet. It ensures the efficient cycling of nutrients, regulates populations and fosters adaptability to environmental changes. As stewards of the Earth, understanding and respecting ecological balance is paramount for sustainable living, as it underlines the interconnectedness of all life forms and the responsibility we bear in maintaining the health and integrity of our shared home.

Biodiversity:

Biodiversity, a cornerstone of ecological balance, encapsulates the richness and variety of life within an ecosystem. It manifests in the diversity of species, genetic variability, and the myriad of ecosystems that collectively form the intricate tapestry of our planet. This diversity is not just a testament to the evolutionary processes that have shaped life over millennia but is also fundamental to the resilience and adaptability of ecosystems.

The presence of a wide array of species within an ecosystem ensures that each organism occupies a unique niche, contributing to the efficient functioning of the entire system. Genetic diversity, on the other hand, provides the raw material for adaptation and evolution, enabling species to cope with changing environmental conditions. Moreover, diverse ecosystems offer multiple services such as pollination, water purification, and climate regulation, essential for the well-being of both wildlife and human populations.

In the face of environmental changes and disturbances, ecosystems with high biodiversity exhibit greater resilience. The redundancy and functional diversity inherent in a biodiverse system enable it to absorb shocks, recover from disturbances, and maintain ecological balance. Recognizing the intrinsic value of biodiversity is not only crucial for the conservation of individual species but is also paramount for fostering sustainable ecosystems that can endure the challenges of an ever-changing world. As stewards of the Earth, it is our responsibility to protect and preserve biodiversity, ensuring the continued health and adaptability of our interconnected natural systems.

Resilience:

Resilience stands as a fundamental attribute of ecosystems, representing their capacity to rebound and adapt in the face of disturbances or changes. The ecological system can absorb shocks, maintain its structure, and continue functioning, showcasing a remarkable capacity for self-restoration. A resilient ecosystem possesses the flexibility and adaptive mechanisms necessary to navigate environmental challenges, ensuring its stability and continuity over time.

In times of disturbance, be it natural events, human activities, or climatic shifts, a resilient ecosystem can absorb the impact without undergoing irreversible damage. This resilience is often rooted in the biodiversity, redundancy, and functional diversity present within the ecosystem. Diverse species and ecological niches contribute to a web of interactions that can compensate for disturbances, preventing the unravelling of the system.

Furthermore, resilient ecosystems are characterized by feedback mechanisms and self-regulating processes that help maintain a balance between various components. These mechanisms enable the ecosystem to recover, regenerate, and adapt, allowing it to persist and function despite external challenges.

Understanding and fostering resilience in ecosystems are critical aspects of conservation and sustainable environmental management. Recognizing the intricate interplay of factors that contribute to resilience empowers us to make informed decisions that safeguard the health and stability of ecosystems, ensuring they continue to provide vital services and support life in the face of an ever-changing world.

Feedback Mechanisms:

Feedback mechanisms are processes that amplify or dampen the effects of changes within an ecosystem. Positive feedback loops enhance and accelerate changes, while negative feedback loops stabilise and regulate the system. Understanding these mechanisms is crucial for maintaining ecological stability.

2.2 Structure and Function of an Ecosystem

2.2.1 Trophic Levels and Energy Flow

Trophic Levels: Trophic levels represent the hierarchical levels in an ecosystem based on an organism's position in the food chain. There are three main trophic levels: producers, consumers, and decomposers.

Producers: These are organisms, mainly plants and some algae, that can produce their food through photosynthesis. They form the base of the food chain by converting sunlight into energy-rich organic compounds.

Consumers: Consumers are organisms that obtain their energy by consuming other living organisms. They are classified into different levels based on their position in the food chain, such as primary consumers (herbivores), secondary consumers (carnivores or omnivores), and tertiary consumers (predators at the top of the food chain).

Decomposers: Decomposers, such as bacteria and fungi, break down dead organic matter and waste, returning nutrients to the soil. They play a crucial role in nutrient recycling.

Energy Flow: Energy flows through trophic levels in an ecosystem. Producers capture solar energy and convert it into chemical energy through photosynthesis. This energy is then transferred through the food chain as consumers feed on one another. However, energy is lost at each trophic level, primarily as heat during metabolic processes, which influences the structure and dynamics of ecosystems.

2.2.2 Nutrient Cycling in Ecosystems

Nutrient Cycles: Nutrient cycling involves the movement and recycling of essential elements, such as carbon, nitrogen, and phosphorus, within an ecosystem. These cycles include processes like photosynthesis, respiration, decomposition, and nutrient uptake by organisms.

Carbon Cycle: Involves the circulation of carbon through the atmosphere, plants, animals, soil, and oceans.

Nitrogen Cycle: Encompasses the conversion of nitrogen between different forms, involving nitrogen-fixing bacteria, plants, and decomposers.

Phosphorus Cycle: Focuses on the movement of phosphorus through rocks, soil, water, and living organisms.

Role of Decomposers: Decomposers break down dead organic matter into simpler compounds, releasing nutrients back into the soil. This nutrient recycling is crucial for maintaining the availability of essential elements for the growth of plants and, consequently, other organisms within the ecosystem.

2.2.3 Biotic and Abiotic Interactions

Biotic Interactions: These are interactions between living organisms within an ecosystem. **Examples** include predation, competition, mutualism, and symbiosis. These interactions shape the population dynamics and diversity of species within an ecosystem.

Abiotic Interactions: Abiotic interactions involve the relationship between living organisms and non-living elements of the environment, such as temperature, water availability, and soil composition. These interactions influence the distribution and behaviour of organisms and play a crucial role in determining the structure and function of ecosystems.

Case Studies: Case studies provide real-world examples of how biotic and abiotic interactions contribute to the structure and function of ecosystems. They illustrate the complex relationships and dependencies that exist within various ecological systems.

2.3 Types of Ecosystems in India

2.3.1 Forest Ecosystem

a) Diversity of Indian Forests

India is home to a rich variety of forest ecosystems, each characterized by unique environmental conditions, vegetation, and wildlife.

The major types of forests in India include:

Tropical Rainforests: Found in regions with high rainfall and temperature, like the Western Ghats and parts of northeastern India. These forests are characterized by dense vegetation and high biodiversity.

Deciduous Forests: Predominant in areas with seasonal rainfall. Trees in these forests shed their leaves during the dry season. Examples include the forests of Central India.

Alpine Forests: Located in mountainous regions at higher altitudes, such as the Himalayas. These forests are adapted to colder climates and have specific flora and fauna suited to alpine conditions.

Highlighting Unique Flora and Fauna: Each type of forest ecosystem in India harbours a distinct set of plant and animal species adapted to its specific ecological conditions. For instance, tropical rainforests may host a variety of exotic plant species and diverse wildlife, while alpine forests may have unique adaptations for survival in harsh mountain environments.

b) Threats and Conservation Measures

Threats to Forests:

1. Deforestation:

a. Agricultural Expansion:

Extent: Large-scale clearing of forests for agriculture, especially for cash crops and monoculture.

Impact: Loss of biodiversity, disruption of ecosystems, and reduction in carbon sequestration capacity.

Mitigation: Sustainable agricultural practices, afforestation, and reforestation initiatives.

2. Illegal Logging:

a. Timber and Wood Trade:

Extent: Unlawful felling of trees for commercial purposes, including timber and wood products.

Impact: Loss of valuable tree species, habitat disruption, and economic losses for legal forestry.

Mitigation: Strict law enforcement, monitoring of timber trade, and community involvement in anti-logging efforts.

3. Habitat Destruction:

a. Urbanization and Infrastructure:

Extent: Conversion of forest land for urban development, roads, and industrial projects.

Impact: Fragmentation of habitats, displacement of wildlife, and alteration of natural landscapes.

Mitigation: Sustainable urban planning, conservation zoning, and restoration of degraded areas.

Conservation and Sustainable Management Efforts:

1. Protected Areas:

a. National Parks and Wildlife Sanctuaries:**

Objective: Preserving critical habitats and providing undisturbed areas for wildlife.

Management: Regulations restricting human activities, scientific research, and wildlife conservation initiatives.

Examples: Jim Corbett National Park, and Sundarbans National Park.

2. Afforestation Programs:

a. Large-Scale Tree Plantation:

Objective: Restoring deforested or degraded areas to enhance biodiversity and ecosystem services.

Initiatives: National Afforestation Program, Green India Mission.

Community Participation: Involving local communities in planting and maintenance.

3. Community Involvement:

a. Sustainable Resource Use:

Awareness Programs: Educating communities on sustainable practices and the importance of biodiversity conservation.

Livelihood Opportunities: Providing alternative livelihoods that reduce dependence on forest resources.

Joint Forest Management (JFM): Collaborative efforts involving local communities in forest protection and management.

b. Traditional Ecological Knowledge:

Recognition: Valuing and incorporating traditional knowledge in forest management decisions.

Conservation Practices: Integrating indigenous practices that promote sustainable resource use.

c. Biodiversity Monitoring and Research:

Scientific Studies: Understanding local biodiversity, species distribution, and ecosystem dynamics.

Conservation Planning: Using research findings to inform conservation strategies and adapt management practices.

Challenges and Future Perspectives:

Land-Use Conflicts: Balancing economic development with conservation priorities.

Climate Change Impacts: Mitigating and adapting to climate-related challenges affecting forest ecosystems.

Policy Implementation: Ensuring effective enforcement of conservation policies.

International Cooperation: Collaborating with neighbouring countries on transboundary conservation efforts.

Sustainable forest management requires a holistic approach that addresses both ecological and socio-economic aspects, involving various stakeholders to ensure the long-term health and resilience of Indian forests.

2.3.2 Grassland Ecosystem

Imagine wide stretches of open land, gently swaying with grass, forming mesmerizing grassland ecosystems. In India, places like the Deccan Plateau boast these vast grassy expanses. These lands are not just scenic beauty; they play a vital role. Grazing animals find their home here, living harmoniously with nature. However, these ecosystems face challenges, with overgrazing being a concern. Striking a balance between nurturing these grasslands and meeting the needs of both wildlife and people is essential. These landscapes, from the Thar Desert to the Eastern Ghats, paint a picture of ecological harmony and the delicate dance of survival.

a) Importance of Grasslands in India

Exploration of Significance: Grasslands in India play a crucial role in the country's ecology and economy. These ecosystems are characterized by a dominance of grasses and herbaceous plants, and they are found in various regions, from the Deccan Plateau to the foothills of the Himalayas.

Biodiversity: Grasslands contribute significantly to biodiversity, providing habitats for a diverse range of plant and animal species. Various grasses, wildflowers, insects, birds, and mammals are adapted to the specific conditions of these ecosystems.

Grazing: Grasslands are essential for grazing animals, including domesticated livestock. Many herbivores depend on grasslands for forage, making these ecosystems important for pastoral communities and the livestock industry.

Agriculture: Some grasslands are converted for agricultural purposes, and they contribute to the production of crops and forage for livestock.

Discussion on Unique Species: Grassland ecosystems in India are home to unique flora and fauna adapted to open landscapes and seasonal changes. This may include species such as various grass species, wildflowers, insects, rodents, ungulates (hoofed mammals), and birds that are specially adapted to the grassland habitat.

b) Grazing Management and Conservation

Examination of Sustainable Grazing Practices: Sustainable grazing practices are essential to maintain the health and productivity of grassland ecosystems.

Rotational Grazing: Systematically moving livestock to different areas, allowing vegetation to recover in previously grazed areas.

Grazing Intensity Management: Monitoring and controlling the number of animals grazing in a particular area to prevent overgrazing.

Impact of Overgrazing: Overgrazing occurs when the intensity and duration of grazing exceed the capacity of the grassland to regenerate. This can lead to degradation of the ecosystem, loss of biodiversity, and soil erosion.

Conservation Efforts:

Conservation efforts aim to preserve grassland biodiversity and ensure sustainable use.

Protected Areas: Establishing reserves and protected areas to safeguard critical grassland habitats and prevent excessive human interference.

Restoration Programs: Initiatives to restore degraded grasslands through reseeding, habitat restoration, and erosion control.

Community Involvement: Engaging local communities in the management and conservation of grasslands, recognising their role in sustainable resource use.

2.3.3 Desert Ecosystem

Envision an expansive expanse of golden sand, where the relentless sun crafts illusions that dance across the horizon—the domain of the desert ecosystem. Within India, the Thar Desert unveils its parched grandeur. In this land of extremes, survival is an art. Specially adapted flora like resilient cacti and tenacious fauna like camels carve out existence. Amidst the adversity, a remarkable biodiversity unfolds, showcasing life forms adept at water conservation. Yet, the human footprint raises concerns, pushing the boundaries of desertification. Safeguarding this fragile equilibrium is imperative, for within these seemingly desolate realms lies a mosaic of life, defiantly flourishing in the limitless stretch of the Indian desert.

a) Characteristics of Indian Deserts

Description of the unique features of Indian deserts, including the Thar Desert. Discussion on adaptations of flora and fauna to arid conditions.

b) Desertification Issues and Mitigation

Analysis of desertification processes in India, addressing factors such as soil erosion and water scarcity. Exploration of mitigation strategies, including water conservation and afforestation.

2.3.4 Aquatic Ecosystems

Embark on a journey through the aquatic landscapes that grace the Indian scenery, where a rich variety of ecosystems comes to life. Ponds, streams, lakes, rivers, oceans, and estuaries unfurl a story of biodiversity. These liquid realms host an assortment of plant and animal life, from microscopic organisms to magnificent marine beings. Yet, challenges emerge—pollution, excessive exploitation, and habitat decline threaten their well-being. Preserving the delicate equilibrium of aquatic ecosystems becomes crucial, calling for sustainable approaches to safeguard their intricate harmony. Amidst these waters, a symphony of life persists, reflecting the enduring spirit of India's aquatic mosaic.

a) Overview of Various Aquatic Ecosystems in India:

Ponds, Streams, Lakes, Rivers, Oceans, Estuaries: India hosts a diverse array of aquatic ecosystems, each with unique characteristics and biodiversity.

Ponds: Small, still-water bodies often found in various landscapes. They can support a variety of aquatic plants and animals.

Streams: Flowing water bodies, typically smaller than rivers, with a continuous flow of water. Streams may be sourced from springs or rainfall.

Lakes: Larger bodies of still water, varying in size and depth. Lakes may be freshwater or saline and support diverse aquatic life.

Rivers: Flowing water bodies with a significant volume of water. Rivers are crucial for transporting nutrients, and they support various aquatic species.

Oceans: Vast bodies of saltwater that cover large portions of the Earth's surface. Oceans host diverse marine life and play a crucial role in regulating the planet's climate.

Estuaries: Transitional zones where rivers meet the sea, characterized by a mix of freshwater and saltwater. Estuaries serve as nurseries for many marine species.

Aquatic ecosystems are vital for both aquatic life and human well-being.

Aquatic Life: These ecosystems support a wide range of plants and animals adapted to aquatic environments. They provide habitats for fish, invertebrates, aquatic plants, and various other organisms.

Human Well-being: Aquatic ecosystems contribute to human well-being by providing water for drinking, agriculture, and industrial use. They also support fisheries, tourism, and recreational activities.

b) Threats to Aquatic Ecosystems:

Aquatic ecosystems face various threats that impact their health and biodiversity.

Pollution: Contamination from industrial discharges, agricultural runoff, and urban waste can degrade water quality.

Overfishing: Excessive and unsustainable fishing practices can deplete fish populations, disrupting the balance of aquatic ecosystems.

Habitat Destruction: Alterations to aquatic habitats, such as dam construction and wetland drainage, can negatively impact biodiversity.

Consequences for Biodiversity and Human Communities: These threats can lead to the loss of biodiversity, decline in fish stocks, and disruption of ecosystem services. Human communities that rely on aquatic resources may suffer from reduced livelihoods, compromised water quality, and loss of cultural and recreational values.

c) Conservation Strategies:

Conservation of Aquatic Ecosystems: Policies, Practices, and Community Involvement

1. Sustainable Fisheries Management:

a. Fishing Quotas:

Objective: Regulating the quantity of fish harvested to prevent overexploitation.

Implementation: Monitoring fish populations, setting catch limits, and issuing fishing permits.

Benefits: Maintaining fish stocks, supporting ecosystem balance, and ensuring long-term fisheries viability.

b. Size Limits:

Objective: Preserving reproductive adults and preventing the capture of undersized individuals.

Implementation: Establishing size restrictions on caught fish through regulations.

Benefits: Promoting natural breeding, sustaining fish populations, and maintaining biodiversity.

c. Seasonal Closures:

Objective: Protecting vulnerable species during critical life stages and breeding seasons.

Implementation: Temporarily closing fishing areas during specific times of the year.

Benefits: Facilitating reproduction, enhancing fish resilience, and supporting ecosystem health.

2. Pollution Control Measures:

a. Industrial and Agricultural Regulations:

Objective: Minimizing pollutants from industrial discharges and agricultural runoff.

Implementation: Enforcing strict regulations, conducting regular inspections, and promoting eco-friendly practices.

Benefits: Reducing water contamination, protecting aquatic life, and ensuring water quality.

b. Wastewater Treatment:

Objective: Treating urban and industrial wastewater to remove contaminants before discharge.

Implementation: Establishing treatment plants, upgrading infrastructure, and promoting proper sewage disposal.

Benefits: Preventing water pollution, safeguarding ecosystems, and promoting public health.

3. Marine Protected Areas:

a. Critical Habitat Protection:

Objective: Safeguarding vital marine habitats like coral reefs, seagrasses, and breeding grounds.

Designation: Identifying and demarcating areas as marine protected zones.

Benefits: Preserving biodiversity, supporting fish spawning, and enhancing ecosystem resilience.

b. Limiting Human Activities:

Objective: Reducing human impact on marine ecosystems within protected areas.

Management Measures: Restricting fishing, shipping, and coastal development.

Benefits: Minimizing habitat disturbance, allowing for natural processes, and maintaining ecosystem integrity.

c. Community Participation:

Local Engagement: Involving coastal communities in the decision-making process.

Traditional Knowledge: Integrating indigenous practices and knowledge in management plans.

Sustainable Livelihoods: Balancing conservation with the socio-economic needs of local communities.

Challenges and Future Strategies:

Illegal, Unreported, and Unregulated (IUU) Fishing: Strengthening monitoring and enforcement mechanisms to combat illegal fishing activities.

Climate Change Impacts: Developing adaptive strategies to address the effects of climate change on aquatic ecosystems.

International Cooperation: Collaborating with neighbouring countries on transboundary conservation efforts.

Education and Awareness: Promoting understanding and appreciation of aquatic ecosystems to garner public support for conservation.

Conserving aquatic ecosystems requires a comprehensive and collaborative approach, involving governments, communities, and stakeholders to balance ecological health with human needs.

References:

1. Sharma, R & Singh, S 2015, 'Forest Ecosystems in India', in JK Patel & NM Gupta (eds.), Biodiversity Conservation and Management, Wiley, Delhi, pp. 110-135.
2. Kumar, A & Patel, M 2019, 'Importance of Grasslands in India', in SK Mishra & RG Sharma (eds.), Grassland Ecology and Management, Cambridge University Press, Cambridge, pp. 45-62.

3. Gupta, N & Singh, A 2017, 'Characteristics of Indian Deserts', in RD Sharma & PK Verma (eds.), Desert Ecosystems: Diversity and Conservation, Oxford University Press, Oxford, pp. 75-92.
4. Patil, V & Rao, S 2021, 'Conservation Strategies for Aquatic Ecosystems', in LM Patel & SK Singh (eds.), Aquatic Ecology: Challenges and Solutions, Springer, New York, pp. 120-140.

CHAPTER THREE

Environmental Pollution

Pollution is the infusion of harmful substances into the environment, disrupting its balance and inflicting damage on ecosystems. This includes air, water, soil, and noise pollution, stemming from human activities like industrial processes, agriculture, and improper waste disposal. The release of pollutants, such as chemicals, particulate matter, and toxins, results in ecological instability, compromising the health of plants, animals, and humans. Beyond immediate harm, pollution leads to long-term environmental disorders, including soil degradation, water contamination, and air quality deterioration. Addressing pollution demands concerted efforts, encompassing regulatory measures, sustainable practices, and public awareness to safeguard the delicate equilibrium of our planet.

Air Pollution

Air pollution refers to the introduction of harmful substances, often in the form of pollutants, into the Earth's atmosphere. These pollutants, which can be gases, particulate matter, biological molecules, or other materials, can have detrimental effects on human health, the environment, and the climate.

Air pollution, casting a foreboding shadow across our skies, emerges from a multitude of origins. Natural phenomena like wildfires and human endeavours, be it industrial discharges or vehicular emissions, collectively contribute to this atmospheric turmoil. Diverse pollutants, encompassing particulate matter, nitrogen oxides, sulphur dioxide, carbon monoxide, ozone, and volatile organic compounds, intricately interlace to create a complex tableau of environmental disruption. The consequences ripple through human well-being and ecosystems alike. To grasp and alleviate this airborne menace, concerted endeavours are essential, spanning stringent regulations for industrial emissions to championing cleaner energy alternatives. It is through collective action that we can reclaim a breath of fresh air for our planet.

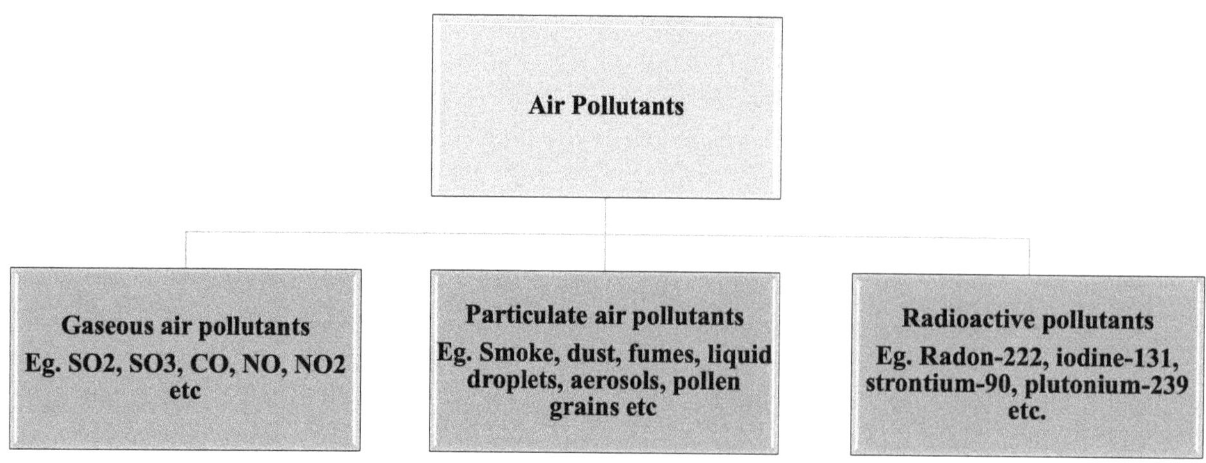

Figure: Classification of Air Pollution

Air pollutants

Primary Pollutants

The substance which is emitted directly from the point source

Eg. SO2, SO3, CO, NO, No2

Radioactive substances etc.

Secondary pollutants

Substances which are formed by the interaction of primary pollutants with other primary pollutants or with some natural constituents of the atmosphere

Eg. Ozone, peroxyacetyl nitrate (PAN), photochemical, smog etc.

Figure: Air Pollutants

3.1.1 Sources and Types of Air Pollutants:

Sources of Air Pollutants:

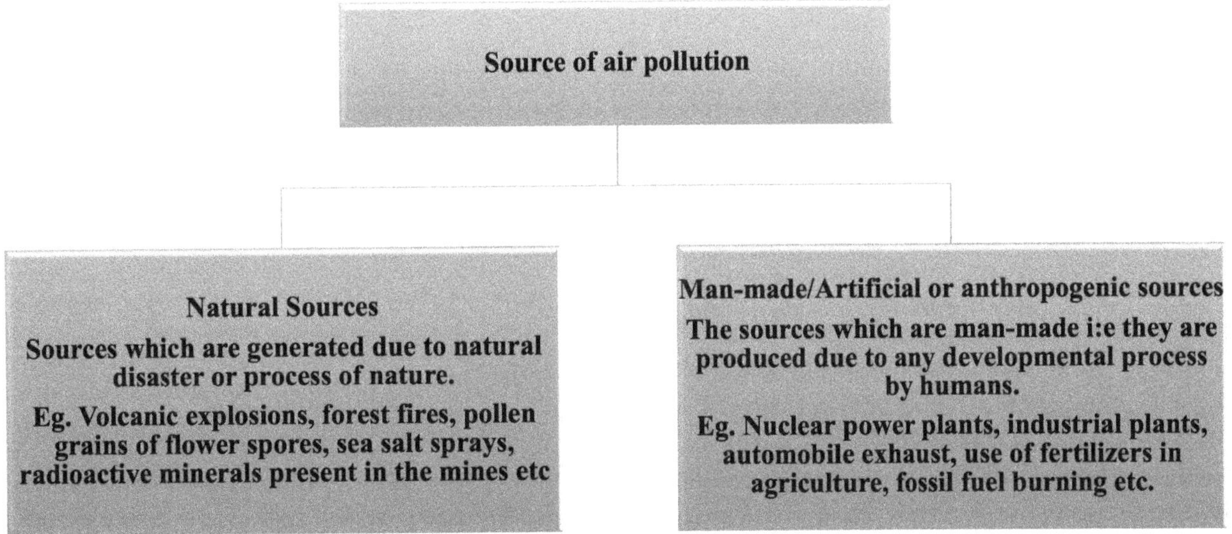

Figure: Sources of Air Pollution

1. Natural Sources:

Wildfires: Natural fires release large amounts of particulate matter and gases, contributing to air pollution. The combustion of vegetation during wildfires releases pollutants such as carbon monoxide and particulate matter into the atmosphere.

Volcanic Activities: Volcanic eruptions release sulphur dioxide, ash, and other pollutants. While volcanic emissions are natural, they can have significant local and even global impacts on air quality.

2. Anthropogenic Sources:

Industries: Emissions from industrial processes release pollutants like particulate matter, sulfur dioxide, nitrogen oxides, and volatile organic compounds into the air. Examples include emissions from factories, power plants, and manufacturing facilities.

Vehicles: Combustion engines in cars, trucks, and other vehicles emit pollutants such as nitrogen oxides, carbon monoxide, and particulate matter. Traffic-related air pollution is a major concern in urban areas.

Agricultural Practices: Agricultural activities contribute to air pollution through the release of ammonia from fertilizers and animal waste. Pesticides and herbicides can also release volatile organic compounds.

Types of Air Pollutants:

1. Particulate Matter (PM):

Sources: Combustion processes (including vehicle engines and industrial activities), construction activities, and natural sources (e.g., wildfires).

Characteristics: Fine particles can penetrate the respiratory system, leading to health issues. Coarse particles can cause respiratory and cardiovascular problems.

Impact: Adverse effects on respiratory health, visibility reduction, and contributions to climate change.

2. Nitrogen Oxides (NOx):

Sources: Combustion processes in vehicles and industrial facilities.

Characteristics: Nitrogen dioxide (NO2) is a common nitrogen oxide.

Impact: Respiratory problems, formation of ground-level ozone, and contribution to acid rain.

3. Sulfur Dioxide (SO2):

Sources: Combustion of fossil fuels, especially coal and oil, in power plants and industrial facilities.

Characteristics: Colorless gas with a pungent odour.

Impact: Respiratory issues, acid rain formation, and damage to vegetation.

4. Carbon Monoxide (CO):

Sources: Incomplete combustion of fossil fuels in vehicles and indoor heating appliances.

Characteristics: Colorless and odourless gas.

Impact: Reduces oxygen transport in the bloodstream, leading to health issues.

1. Ozone (O3):

Sources: Formation in the atmosphere due to reactions between nitrogen oxides and volatile organic compounds in the presence of sunlight.

Characteristics: A major component of smog.

Impact: Respiratory problems, harm to vegetation and contributes to the greenhouse effect.

6. Volatile Organic Compounds (VOCs):

Sources: Emissions from industrial processes, vehicle exhaust, and certain household products.

Characteristics: Organic chemicals that easily vaporize into the air.

Impact: Contributes to the formation of ground-level ozone and can have adverse health effects.

3.1.2 Air Quality Standards in India

National Ambient Air Quality Standards (NAAQS)

Provide an overview of the air quality standards set by regulatory bodies in India. Discuss permissible limits for key pollutants and how these standards aim to protect public health and the environment.

Monitoring and Assessment

Explain the methods and technologies used to monitor air quality, including air quality index (AQI) systems. Discuss the importance of real-time monitoring and how data is utilized for policymaking.

3.1.3 Control Measures and Policies

Regulatory Framework

Explore the regulatory framework in India for controlling air pollution, including acts, rules, and agencies responsible for enforcement.

Control Measures

Discuss technological solutions and best practices for controlling air pollution, such as emission control devices, fuel quality improvements, and promoting public transportation. Highlight successful case studies and policy interventions.

Effects of Air Pollution

Sr No.	Type of Effect	Example
1	Effects on human health	• Long-term exposure to air pollutants e.g. cigarette smoke, automobile exhaustion, SO2, NO2 etc. • adversely affect the natural defences of the respiratory system (hairs and sticky mucus in the lining of the nose) leading to lung cancer, asthma, chronic bronchitis, shortness of breath etc. • Long exposure to CO leads to suffocation, dizziness, unconsciousness and even death due to the formation of carboxyhaemoglobin.
2	Effects on plants	• Bleaching of leaves, chlorosis, injury and necrosis of leaves due to SO. • NO2 results in increased cutting off and repressed growth of plants. • Specks on the leaf surface, premature ageing, necrosis and bleaching are caused by ozone. • Necrosis of leaf-tip by Fluorides.
3	Effects on aquatic or marine life	• Air pollutants can cause acid rain by mixing with rainwater. • Acid rain pollutes fresh water lakes, damaging aquatic or marine life.
4	Effects on material	• Particulate air pollutants are corrosive in nature and hence cause damage to exposed metal surfaces like metal parts of buildings, vehicles, bridges, wires, metallic tracks etc. • The presence of SO2 and moisture can enhance the corrosion of metallic, surfaces due to the formation of sulphuric acid. • SO can affect fabric, leather, paint and even paper.
5	Global warming	• The environment has a gentle equilibrium of naturally occurring gases that trap some of the sun's heat near the earth's surface. • This "greenhouse effect" keeps the Earth's temperature stable. • Unfortunately, humans have troubled this natural equilibrium by producing huge quantities of some of these greenhouse gases, like carbon dioxide and methane. • As a result, the Earth's atmosphere seems to be trapping more of the sun's heat, causing the Earth's average temperature to increase- a phenomenon known as global warming.

Effect of Air Pollution

Indoor Air Pollution-Present Scenario

In recent times, pollution has emerged as a pressing issue, and one of the significant contributors is radon gas. This particular gas takes center stage as the foremost indoor air pollutant, and its radioactive byproducts are responsible for a substantial number of lung cancer cases each year. Radon primarily finds its way into indoor environments through construction materials like bricks, concrete, and tiles. These materials, being derived from soil containing radium, contribute to the presence of radon gas indoors.

Moreover, sources such as groundwater and natural gas also harbor radon, and when these resources are utilized, the gas is emitted into the surrounding environment. This poses a significant health risk, as prolonged exposure to radon and its radioactive offspring can lead to severe health issues, particularly lung cancer.

In the context of developing countries, including India, a noteworthy source of indoor air pollution is the continued use of traditional fuels for domestic purposes. Despite the advancements in technology, many people in these regions still rely on coal, dung-cakes, wood, and kerosene for cooking and heating. The incomplete combustion of these fuels produces toxic gases, with carbon monoxide (CO) being a prominent example. This gas is known for its harmful effects on human health, especially when inhaled in enclosed spaces.

Burning coal, a common practice in these regions, also results in the emission of sulfur dioxide (SO2). The sulfur content in coal varies, and when it combusts, it releases SO2 into the atmosphere. This sulfur dioxide contributes to air pollution and can lead to respiratory issues, including aggravating conditions such as asthma.

In essence, the reliance on certain construction materials and traditional fuels in both developed and developing regions significantly impacts air quality, posing health risks to individuals exposed to the pollutants emitted. Addressing these sources and promoting cleaner alternatives is crucial in mitigating the adverse effects on both indoor and outdoor air quality.

Reduction of Air Pollution through Devices/ Equipment

Air pollution is a significant environmental concern, and various technologies have been developed to mitigate the emission of pollutants into the atmosphere. Here, we will discuss four important devices or equipment - Cyclones, Bag House Filters, Wet Scrubbers, and Electrostatic Precipitators - that play crucial roles in reducing air pollution.

1. Cyclones:

Principle:

Cyclones operate on the principle of centrifugal force to separate particulate matter from an air or gas stream. The polluted air enters a cylindrical or conical chamber tangentially, creating a high-velocity vortex within the chamber. This vortex imparts centrifugal force to the suspended particles, causing them to move outward towards the outer wall due to their inertia. As the particles lose their momentum, they settle at the bottom of the cyclone, while the cleaned air exits through the top.

The key components of a cyclone include the inlet duct, the cyclonic chamber, and an outlet for clean air. The efficiency of a cyclone is influenced by factors such as the inlet velocity, cyclone size, and the density of the particles being separated.

Applications:

1. **Woodworking:** Cyclones are employed in woodworking facilities to capture sawdust and other coarse wood particles generated during cutting, shaping, or sanding processes.

2. **Metal Grinding:** Industries involved in metal grinding, machining, or abrasive processes utilize cyclones to capture larger metal particles and dust generated during these operations.

3. **Cement Production:** Cyclones are integral to the dust collection systems in cement plants, efficiently removing larger particles such as cement kiln dust or clinker particles.

Advantages:

1. **Simplicity:** Cyclones are relatively simple in design, consisting of few moving parts. This simplicity contributes to their robustness and ease of operation.

2. **Cost-Effectiveness:** Cyclones are cost-effective to install and maintain, making them an attractive choice for industries with coarse particle emissions, especially when compared to more complex and expensive air pollution control technologies.

3. **Low Maintenance Requirements:** Due to their simple design, cyclones have low maintenance needs. Regular inspections, occasional cleaning, and checking for any wear or corrosion are typically sufficient to ensure proper functioning.

4. **High-Temperature Handling:** Cyclones can handle high temperatures, making them suitable for applications where the air or gas stream may be hot, such as in metal smelting or certain industrial processes.

5. **Large Particle Removal:** Cyclones are particularly effective at capturing and removing larger particles from the air stream. This makes them well-suited for industries where coarse particulate matter is a primary concern.

Design Variations: Cyclones come in various designs, including single-cylinder, multiple-cylinder, and conical configurations. The choice of design depends on the specific application and the characteristics of the particulate matter to be separated. Modifications such as the addition of secondary air inlets or vortex finders can enhance cyclone efficiency.

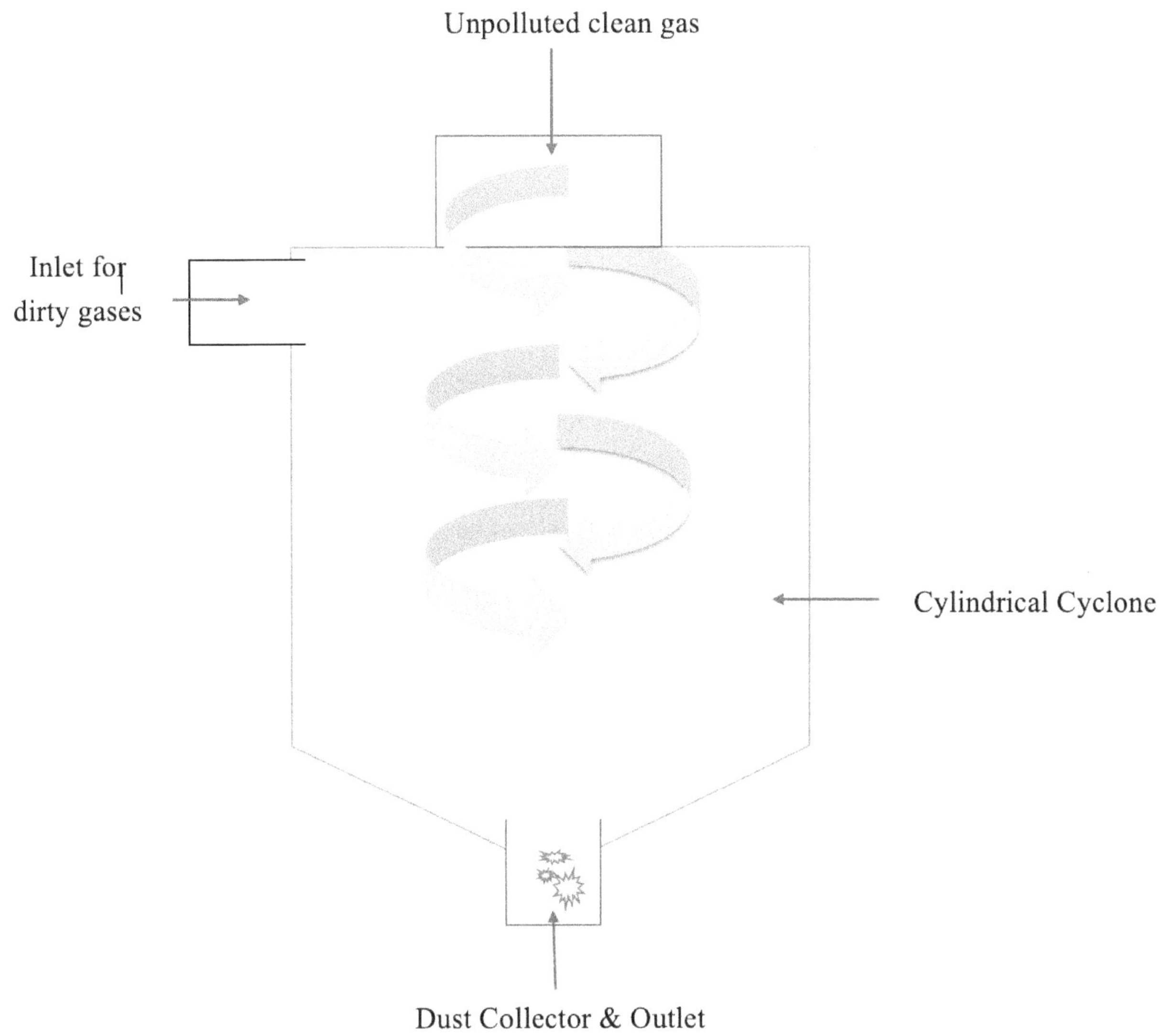

Fig 1: Cyclone Separator

2. Bag House Filters:

Principle:

Bag house filters operate based on the principle of using fabric bags as the filtering medium to capture dust and particulate matter from an incoming air or gas stream. The polluted air enters the bag house and passes through the fabric bags. The fabric material can be made from various materials, such as woven or felted fibres, with specific characteristics tailored to the application.

As the air moves through the fabric bags, the particles within the air stream adhere to the surface of the bags or are trapped within the fabric material. The cleaned air exits through the outlet, leaving the captured particulate matter within the bags. Periodically, during the cleaning cycle, the bags are cleaned to remove accumulated dust, ensuring the continued efficiency of the filtration process.

Applications:

1. **Power Plants:** Bag houses are crucial components in power plants for controlling emissions from boiler and

combustion processes, capturing fine ash particles, and preventing their release into the atmosphere.

2. Cement Production: In the cement industry, bag house filters are employed to capture fine dust generated during various stages of the production process, such as grinding, kiln operations, and material handling.

3. Pharmaceutical Manufacturing: Bag house filters play a vital role in the pharmaceutical industry, where maintaining a clean and sterile environment is crucial. They are used to control particulate emissions from various manufacturing processes.

4. Metal Processing: Industries involved in metal processing, including welding and cutting operations, utilize bag house filters to capture fine metal dust and fumes, ensuring a cleaner and safer working environment.

Advantages:

1. High Efficiency in Fine Particle Collection: Bag house filters excel in capturing fine particles, providing high filtration efficiency and contributing to compliance with stringent environmental standards.

2. Large Surface Area: The design of bag house filters incorporates a large surface area due to the arrangement of multiple fabric bags. This large filtration area enhances their particle-capturing capacity and extends the time between cleaning cycles.

3. Versatility and Customization: Bag house filters are versatile and can be customized to meet specific industrial requirements. Different fabrics, configurations, and sizes can be chosen based on the characteristics of the particulate matter and the operating conditions of the particular application.

4. High-Temperature Handling: Bag house filters can withstand high temperatures, making them suitable for applications where the air or gas stream may carry hot particulate matter, such as in metal smelting or industrial combustion processes.

Design Variations: Bag house filters come in various designs, including pulse jet, reverse air, and shaker types. Each design has its advantages and limitations, and the selection depends on factors such as the application, particulate characteristics, and required operating conditions. Pulse jet bag house filters, for example, use compressed air pulses to dislodge accumulated dust from the bags, enhancing cleaning efficiency.

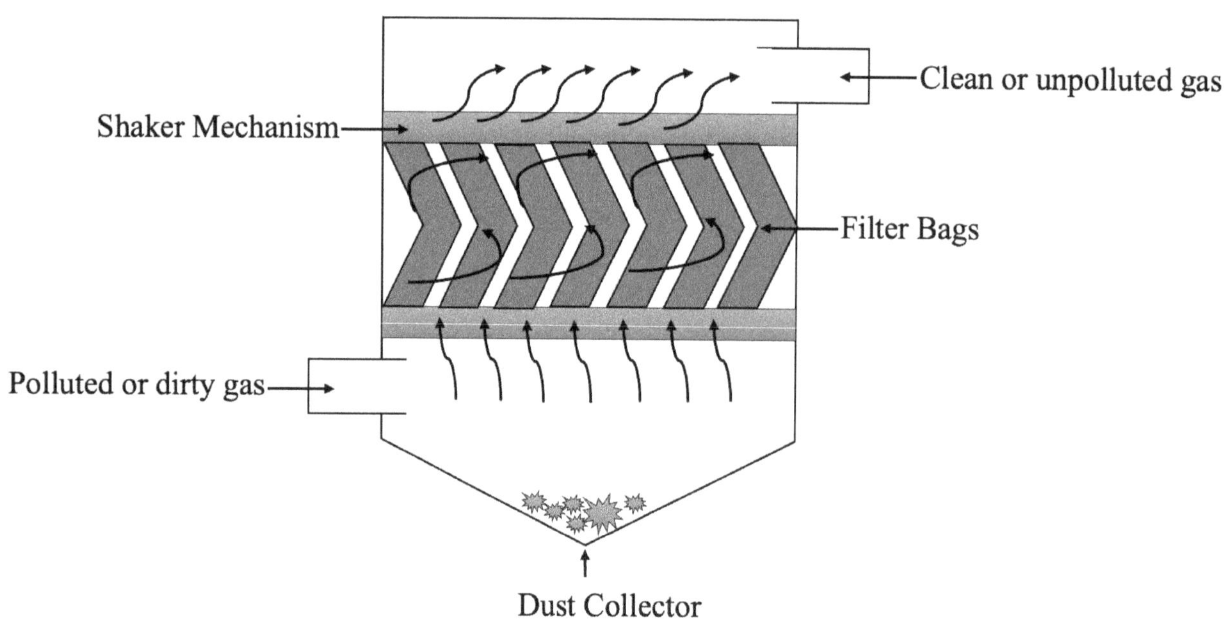

Fig 2: Bag House Filter

3. Wet Scrubbers:

Principle:

Wet scrubbers operate on the principle of using liquid (typically water) to capture and remove pollutants from an air or gas stream. The contaminated air is introduced into a scrubbing chamber, and within this chamber, water droplets are dispersed. The pollutants present in the air, including particulate matter and gases, come into contact with the water droplets. The water effectively captures and absorbs the pollutants, forming a mixture that is then collected and removed from the system. The now-cleaned air is released into the atmosphere.

There are various types of wet scrubbers, including venturi scrubbers, spray tower scrubbers, and packed bed scrubbers, each with specific designs and applications.

Applications:

1. **Chemical Manufacturing:** Wet scrubbers are widely used in chemical plants to control emissions of hazardous gases and particulates generated during various chemical processes.

2. **Metal Processing:** Industries involved in metal processing, such as foundries and smelters, utilize wet scrubbers to capture and remove particulate matter and metal fumes released during high-temperature operations.

3. **Power Generation:** Wet scrubbers play a significant role in power plants, particularly in the control of sulfur dioxide (SO2) emissions from the combustion of fossil fuels. They are effective in removing acidic gases.

4. **Pulp and Paper Industry:** Wet scrubbers are employed in pulp and paper mills to control emissions from processes like pulping and bleaching, where various pollutants are released.

Advantages:

1. **Versatility in Pollutant Removal:** Wet scrubbers are versatile and can effectively remove both particulate matter and gases. This versatility makes them suitable for a wide range of industrial applications where different pollutants may be present.

2. **High Efficiency in Gas Removal:** Wet scrubbers excel in the removal of acidic gases and other gaseous pollutants. They are particularly effective in controlling emissions from high-temperature processes, such as those found in power plants and metal processing facilities.

3. **Cooling Effect:** Wet scrubbers provide a cooling effect on the air stream, which can be beneficial in applications where temperature control is important. This cooling effect can also enhance the efficiency of certain industrial processes.

4. **Flexible Design:** Wet scrubbers come in various designs, allowing for customization based on specific industrial requirements. Different types of wet scrubbers may be chosen based on factors such as the type of pollutants to be controlled, gas volume, and space constraints.

Operational Considerations: Proper maintenance of wet scrubbers is crucial to ensure their long-term performance. Regular checks on liquid flow rates, pH levels, and the condition of scrubber internals are necessary. Monitoring and managing the disposal of the collected wastewater or slurry is essential to comply with environmental regulations.

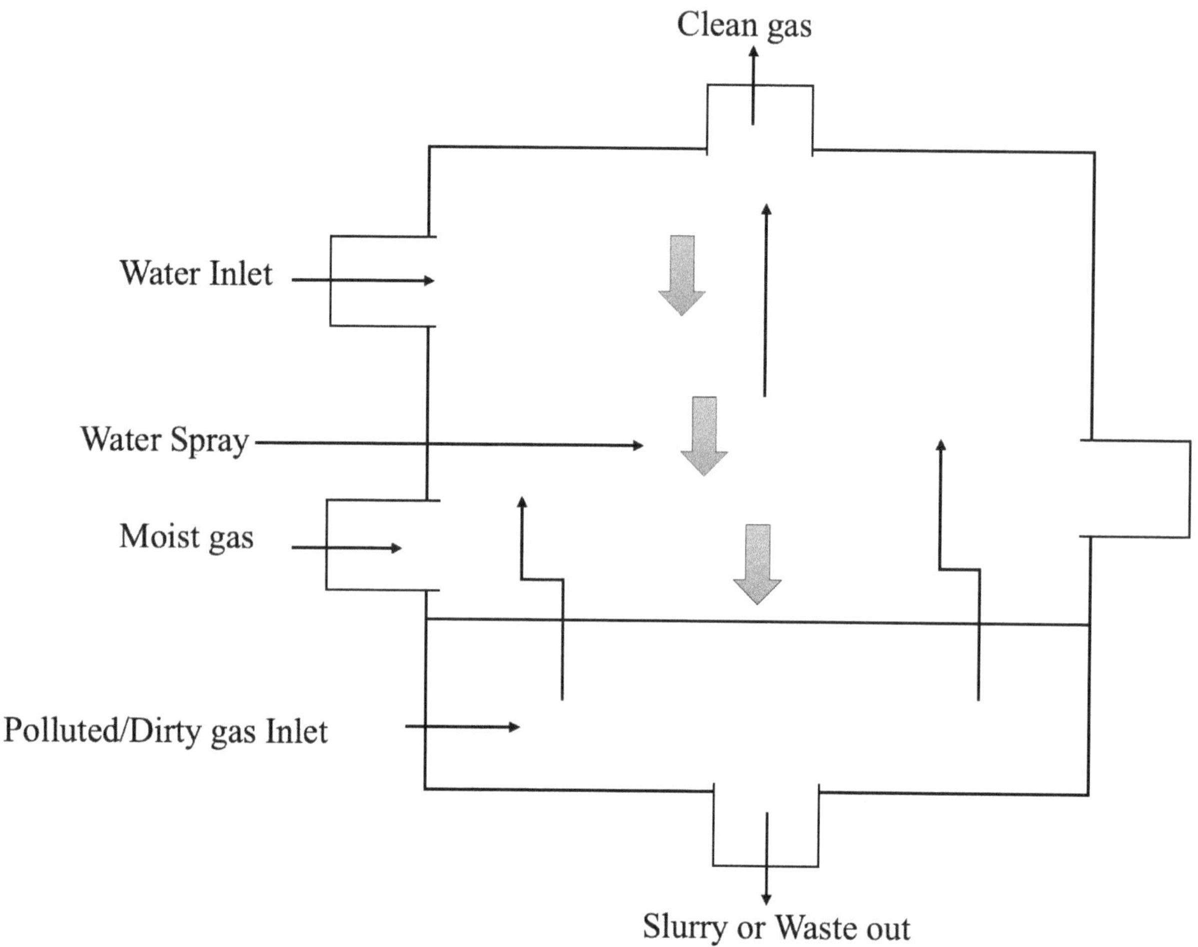

Fig 3: Wet Scrubbers

4. Electrostatic Precipitators:

Principle:

Electrostatic precipitators (ESPs) operate on the principle of using an electric charge to ionize particles in the air. The polluted air stream passes through a series of high-voltage electrodes, where a corona discharge generates ions. These ions impart an electric charge to the particles in the air, creating charged particles. The charged particles are then attracted to oppositely charged collection plates or electrodes, where they adhere and are effectively removed from the air stream. The now-cleaned air is released into the atmosphere.

The key components of an electrostatic precipitator include the discharge electrodes, collecting plates, and a high-voltage power supply.

Applications:

1. Power Plants: ESPs are commonly used in power plants to control emissions from the combustion of fossil fuels, such as coal or oil. They effectively capture fine ash particles, preventing their release into the atmosphere.

2. Steel Mills: In steel manufacturing processes, electrostatic precipitators are employed to control emissions from various operations, including the handling and processing of raw materials and the combustion of fuels.

3. Incinerators: ESPs are utilized in waste incineration facilities to control the release of fine ash and particulate matter generated during the combustion of municipal solid waste.

Advantages:

1. High Efficiency in Fine Particle Removal: Electrostatic precipitators are highly efficient in removing fine particles, including those with submicron sizes. This high efficiency contributes to compliance with stringent emission standards and helps in maintaining clean air.

2. Low-Pressure Drops: ESPs typically have low-pressure drops, meaning they do not significantly impede the flow of the air or gas stream. This characteristic reduces the energy consumption associated with the operation of the precipitator.

3. Handling High Gas Volumes: Electrostatic precipitators can handle large gas volumes, making them suitable for applications where substantial amounts of air or gas need to be processed. This capability is advantageous in industries with high-volume emissions.

4. Effective in High-Temperature Processes: ESPs are especially effective for controlling emissions from high-temperature processes, such as those encountered in power plants or certain industrial furnaces. The robust design of ESPs allows them to withstand elevated temperatures.

5. Minimal Maintenance: Compared to some other air pollution control devices, electrostatic precipitators generally require minimal maintenance. Regular checks on the electrical components and periodic cleaning of the collection plates are typically sufficient to ensure optimal performance.

Design Variations: Electrostatic precipitators come in different designs, including plate-type and tubular precipitators. The choice of design depends on the specific application and the characteristics of the particulate matter to be controlled. Tubular precipitators, for instance, provide a more compact design and are suitable for applications with space constraints.

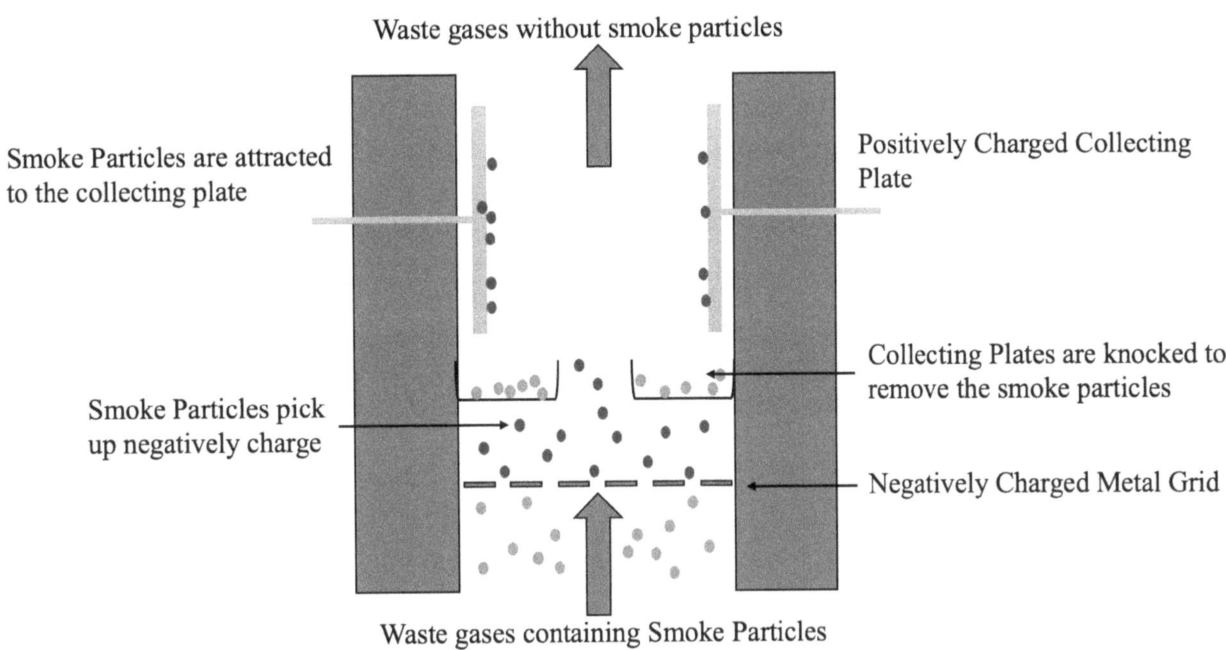

Fig 4: Electrostatic Precipitators

Governmental Acts Related to Air Pollution in India

1. Air (Prevention and Control of Pollution) Act, 1981: The Air Act is a crucial piece of legislation that empowers the Central and State Pollution Control Boards to prevent, control, and abate air pollution. It provides the legal framework for regulating emissions from industries, automobiles, and other sources.

2. Environment (Protection) Act, 1986: The Environment Act grants the central government the authority to take measures to protect and improve environmental quality. Under this act, the Central Pollution Control Board (CPCB) has been established to coordinate environmental protection activities.

3. National Ambient Air Quality Standards (NAAQS): The NAAQS are guidelines set by the Central Pollution Control Board (CPCB) under the Air Act to specify the permissible levels of various pollutants in the ambient air. These standards serve as the benchmark for assessing air quality across the country.

4. Motor Vehicles Act, 1988: The Motor Vehicles Act contains provisions related to vehicular emissions and aims to regulate the standards for vehicle pollution. It empowers authorities to prescribe emission norms and standards for different categories of vehicles.

5. Bharat Stage Emission Standards: Bharat Stage emission standards are set by the Central Government to regulate the emission of air pollutants from internal combustion engine-equipped vehicles. These standards are based on European emission norms and aim to progressively reduce vehicle emissions.

6. National Clean Air Programme (NCAP): Launched in 2019, the NCAP is a comprehensive action plan to address air pollution in various cities across India. It aims to achieve a significant reduction in air pollution levels and includes city-specific action plans, source-wise reduction targets, and a robust monitoring framework.

7. Graded Response Action Plan (GRAP): GRAP is a set of emergency measures to be implemented when air quality reaches severe levels. It includes measures such as restricting vehicular movement, regulating industrial activities, and implementing measures to control dust.

8. Forest (Conservation) Act, 1980: The Forest Act plays a role in protecting the environment, as forests are crucial for maintaining ecological balance and air quality. The act regulates the diversion of forest land for non-forest purposes.

Water Pollution

Water pollution is a significant environmental concern characterized by the introduction of harmful contaminants into water bodies, such as rivers, lakes, oceans, and groundwater. These contaminants, originating from various human activities and natural processes, can compromise the quality of water and pose serious threats to aquatic ecosystems, wildlife, and human health.

Water pollution, a dire consequence of human activities, pervades aquatic realms with a sinister impact. It stems from diverse sources: industrial discharges, agricultural runoff laden with pesticides and nutrients, and untreated urban sewage. This perilous concoction infiltrates rivers, lakes, and oceans, jeopardizing ecosystems and human health. Pathogens, heavy metals, and chemicals weave a tapestry of contamination. The consequences are profound—diminished water quality, aquatic biodiversity loss, and threats to public health. A comprehensive response demands robust regulations, sustainable agricultural practices, and advanced wastewater treatment. Only through collective commitment can we purify the lifeblood of our planet, ensuring water's pristine flow for generations to come.

Sr No.	Pollutants	Sources of pollutants	Effects
1	Pathogens	Sewage, human and animal wastes, natural and domestics overflow from land, industrial waste.	Water-borne diseases (cholera, typhoid, dysentery etc.) deficiency of oxygen.
2	Organic pollutants like oil, grease, soaps, plastics, detergents, fertilizers and pesticides	Automobile and machine tanker leakage, industrial and domestic wastes.	Disruption of aquatic life, genetic defects, mutations, cancer, eutrophication.
3	Inorganic pollutants, phosphates, nitrates, acids and alkalies	Agricultural overflow, mine drainage, domestic and industrial wastes, natural wastes.	Algal bloom and eutrophication, methemoglobinemia, water becomes unsuitable for drinking, irrigation and industrial use.
4	Radioactive wastes	Natural sources, Uranium mining and processing, radioisotopes from hospitals and research laboratories.	Genetic defects, mutations, cancer
5	Thermal waste	Cooling water for industrial, nuclear and thermal plants.	Decrease in solubility of oxygen in water, disruption of aquatic ecosystem.
6	Sediments	Natural erosion, soil, silt, overflows from agricultural land and construction sites	Affects water quality,disruption of aquatic life.

Figure: Sources and effects of some common water pollutants

3.2.1 Major Water Pollutants in India:

Point and Non-point Sources:

1. Point Sources:

Industrial Discharges: Factories and industrial facilities release pollutants directly into water bodies. These pollutants may include heavy metals, chemicals, and other contaminants.

Municipal Wastewater: Discharge from sewage treatment plants and inadequate sanitation systems contribute to water pollution.

2. Non-point Sources:

Agricultural Runoff: The use of fertilizers and pesticides in agriculture can lead to the runoff of nutrients and chemicals into water bodies.

Urban Stormwater: Rainwater runoff in urban areas can carry pollutants such as oil, heavy metals, and debris into rivers and lakes.

Specific Pollutants:

1. **Pathogens:** Bacteria, viruses, and other microorganisms from human and animal waste.
2. **Nutrients:** Excessive levels of nitrogen and phosphorus from fertilizers, lead to eutrophication.
3. **Heavy Metals:** Mercury, lead, cadmium, and arsenic, often originating from industrial discharges.
4. **Chemicals:** Pesticides, herbicides, and industrial chemicals that can contaminate water.

3.2.2 Water Quality Standards and Monitoring:

Drinking Water Standards:

Bureau of Indian Standards (BIS): BIS sets the standards for drinking water quality in India.

Permissible Limits: Standards specify permissible limits for parameters like pH, turbidity, total coliforms, and concentrations of contaminants such as arsenic and fluoride.

Monitoring and Surveillance:

Methodologies: In situ monitoring involves on-site measurements, while laboratory-based techniques analyze water samples for various parameters.

Organizations Involved:

Central Pollution Control Board (CPCB): Governmental body responsible for water quality assessment.

Non-Governmental Organizations (NGOs): Organizations like Greenpeace and WaterAid contribute to monitoring and raising awareness.

3.2.3 Wastewater Treatment:

Wastewater treatment stands as a pivotal shield against environmental degradation, encompassing a spectrum of processes designed to cleanse water tainted by human activities before its return to the environment. As communities burgeon and industries thrive, the volume of wastewater burgeons is laden with pollutants. Treatment facilities employ a gamut of physical, chemical, and biological methods to purify water, ensuring it meets stringent quality standards. Sedimentation, filtration, and biological degradation play vital roles in this purification symphony. With growing global awareness of water scarcity and pollution, wastewater treatment emerges as a linchpin in sustainable water management, exemplifying the intersection of technology, ecology, and public health.

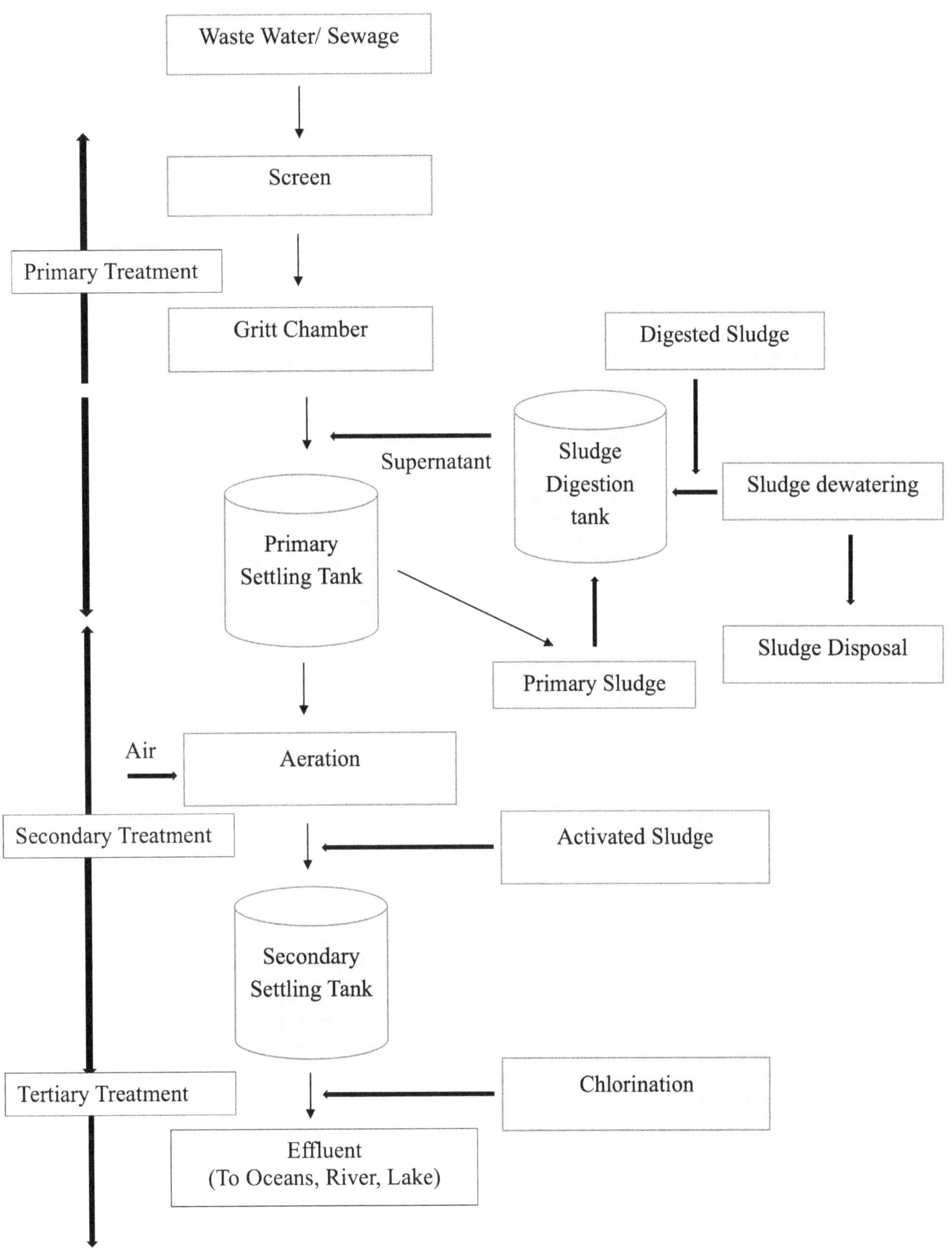

Figure: Waste Water/Sewage Treatment

Treatment Processes:

1. Physical Treatment:

- **Sedimentation:**

In cleaning up dirty water, sedimentation is like a magic trick. Imagine the water going into a big tank. The heavy stuff in the water, like dirt and yucky things, sinks to the bottom of the tank because of gravity, creating a sludgy layer. This helps get rid of the bad stuff, making the water clearer. Sometimes, we use special chemicals to help the dirt clump together. Sedimentation is like the first superhero in cleaning water – it removes the heavy, icky things and makes the water ready for the next steps. It's like a big cleaning hug for the water!

Process: Allows particles to settle at the tank bottom.

Purpose: Separates solid particles from wastewater.

- **Filtration:**

Picture cleaning water like making it run through a giant strainer. In wastewater treatment, filtration is our superhero strainer. So, after sedimentation does its job, the water passes through different layers of sand, gravel, and other materials. These layers act like filters, trapping tiny particles and remaining impurities. It's like when you use a sieve to separate pasta from water but on a much larger scale. Filtration makes sure even the tiniest specks are caught, leaving us with water that's way cleaner and ready for the final touches. So, filtration is our water's superhero sidekick, ensuring it sparkles and shines!

Process: Removes suspended solids using materials like sand.

Purpose: Further filtration to clarify water.

3. Chemical Treatment:

Imagine enchanting water with a powerful elixir to transform it into a pristine marvel – that's the enchantment of chemical treatment in the realm of wastewater purification! Following the filtration process, certain elusive particles may persist in a game of hide-and-seek. This is where the magic of chemicals comes into play. We introduce special elixirs that cause these particles to unite, forming a formidable alliance, much like a superhero team assembling. Once gathered, removing them becomes a breeze. It's akin to adding soap to a soiled dish – the dirt binds together, simplifying the rinsing process. Chemical treatment ensures our water emerges crystal clear, devoid of any lingering mischief, and ready for new escapades!

- **Coagulation-Flocculation:**

The Coagulation-Flocculation assumes a pivotal role, comparable to orchestrating a splendid ball for wayward dancers. Envision minuscule particles in water as playful dancers dispersed in disarray. Enter the "Coagulant," a skilled choreographer. It gracefully dispenses a magical elixir, prompting these unruly dancers to join hands and form graceful pairs, known as "flocs." These flocs resemble well-coordinated dance couples that gracefully settle, leaving the water impeccably clear, akin to the serene aftermath of a captivating dance. Coagulation-Flocculation transforms the water ballet into a seamless spectacle, ensuring a pristine and delightful aquatic performance!

Process: Chemicals induce particles to clump for easier removal.

Purpose: Aggregation of particles for effective separation.

- **Disinfection:**

In wastewater treatment, Disinfection emerges as the grand finale, akin to casting a protective enchantment over the water stage. Picture the water as a bustling theatre, its characters being unseen microorganisms. As the curtains draw to a close, the "Disinfector" takes the spotlight. Armed with chlorine or other potent spells, it graciously eradicates any lingering villain pathogens ensuring a safe and hygienic conclusion to the water's performance. Disinfection, the grand maestro, orchestrates the last act, leaving the water pristine and ready for its next captivating performance in the grand theatre of environmental stewardship.

Process: Chlorination or other methods to kill pathogens.

Purpose: Eliminates harmful microorganisms.

4. Biological Treatment:

In wastewater treatment, Biological Treatment is like the conductor leading a team of tiny cleaners—microorganisms. It's like an orchestra of microbes working together to break down the yucky stuff in water. Picture it as a lively dance where the microbes do their magic. The activated sludge process is a superstar in this dance, making sure everything is in harmony. And there's a peaceful scene with constructed wetlands playing a part too. This natural performance is a great example of how nature cleans water like a magical concert making our environment healthier. So, Biological Treatment is like the boss, directing this awesome orchestra of microbes!

- **Activated Sludge Process:**

In the wastewater treatment spectacle, the Activated Sludge Process takes centre stage. Picture it as a bustling city of microorganisms, each with a role in purifying water. Wastewater, teeming with pollutants, enters this microbial metropolis. Microbes, like busy workers, gobble up the contaminants, transforming the water into something cleaner. It's like a bustling factory where the activated sludge, a mix of microbes and organic matter, works tirelessly to break down pollutants. This natural cleaning process ensures that the water leaving the treatment plant is much cleaner and ready to rejoin nature's flow. The Activated Sludge Process: nature's bustling purification hub!

Process: Microorganisms break down organic matter.

Purpose: Biological decomposition of pollutants.

- **Constructed Wetlands:**

The Constructed Wetlands where nature works its magic to clean up dirty water. It's like a beautiful garden where water filled with impurities comes in. The plants and tiny creatures in the water work together like superheroes. The plants use their roots to clean the water, and the tiny creatures break down the bad stuff. It's like a dance of cleaning! As a result, the water that leaves this special garden is much cleaner and better. Constructed Wetlands show us how nature can turn dirty water into something pure and lovely.

Process: Natural processes in artificial wetlands.

Purpose: Mimics natural purification in wetland ecosystems.

Applicability and Challenges in India:

Applicability:

Adaptation: Technologies must align with the scale and nature of pollution sources.

Context-Sensitivity: Tailoring solutions to diverse wastewater scenarios.

Challenges:

Limited Infrastructure: Insufficient facilities for comprehensive treatment.

Resource Constraints: Financial and technical limitations for widespread adoption.

Decentralization Need: Rural areas lack centralized solutions, requiring decentralized approaches.

Policy Initiatives:

- **Water (Prevention and Control of Pollution) Act, 1974:**

Objective: Framework for preventing and controlling water pollution.

Implementation: Regulatory measures and standards enforcement.

- **National Mission for Clean Ganga (Namami Gange):**

  Objective: Rejuvenate the Ganges and tributaries through pollution control.
  Approach: Focus on wastewater treatment and holistic river management.
  Importance of Public Awareness:

- **Educational Campaigns:**

  Focus: Promoting responsible water use and pollution prevention.
  Impact: Increasing awareness of individual roles in water conservation.

- **Community Participation:**

  Involvement: Engaging local communities in safeguarding water resources.
  Empowerment: Communities actively contribute to water protection efforts.

Understanding water pollutants, monitoring standards, treatment technologies, and policy initiatives is pivotal for sustainable water management in India. Addressing challenges and fostering public awareness are integral to achieving effective wastewater treatment and ensuring the longevity of water resources.

Marine Pollution:

Marine pollution refers to the introduction of harmful substances into the marine environment, leading to adverse effects on the ecosystem and its inhabitants. It is a pressing global issue that poses significant threats to biodiversity, human health, and the overall balance of marine ecosystems. Various human activities contribute to marine pollution, and understanding its causes, effects, and potential solutions is crucial for the preservation of our oceans.

Effect of some common water pollutants

Sr No.	Pollutants	Sources of pollutants	Effects
1	Pathogens	Sewage, human and animal wastes, natural and domestics overflow from land, industrial waste.	Water-borne diseases (cholera, typhoid, dysentery etc.) deficiency of oxygen.
2	Organic pollutants like oil, grease, soaps, plastics, detergents, fertilizers and pesticides	Automobile and machine tanker leakage, industrial and domestic wastes.	Disruption of aquatic life, genetic defects, mutations, cancer, eutrophication.
3	Inorganic pollutants, phosphates, nitrates, acids and alkali	Agricultural overflow, mine drainage, domestic and industrial wastes, natural wastes.	Algal bloom and eutrophication, methemoglobinemia, water becomes unsuitable for drinking, irrigation and industrial use.
4	Radioactive wastes	Natural sources, Uranium mining and processing, radioisotopes from hospitals and research laboratories.	Genetic defects, mutations, cancer
5	Thermal waste	Cooling water for industrial, nuclear and thermal plants.	Decrease in solubility of oxygen in water, disruption of aquatic ecosystem.
6	Sediments	Natural erosion, soil, silt, overflows from agricultural land and construction sites	Affects water quality, disruption of aquatic life.

Effect of Common water pollutants

Causes of Marine Pollution:

1. **Oil Spills:** Accidental or intentional discharges of oil into the oceans pose a severe threat. Oil spills can result from maritime accidents, leakage during oil extraction and transport, or illegal dumping.

2. **Plastic Pollution:** Improper disposal and inadequate waste management have led to a significant increase in plastic debris in the oceans. This includes items like plastic bags, bottles, and microplastics, which can have detrimental effects on marine life.

3. **Chemical Runoff:** Agricultural runoff, industrial discharges, and improper disposal of chemicals contribute to the contamination of marine waters. Pesticides, fertilizers, and industrial chemicals can disrupt marine ecosystems and harm aquatic organisms.

4. **Heavy Metals:** Industrial activities release heavy metals such as mercury, lead, and cadmium into the oceans. These toxic substances accumulate in marine organisms, posing threats to both marine life and human consumers.

5. **Sewage and Nutrient Pollution:** Improperly treated sewage and excessive nutrient runoff from agriculture can lead to nutrient enrichment in coastal waters. This can result in harmful algal blooms, oxygen depletion, and the creation of dead zones.

6. **Shipping Activities:** Ballast water discharge, oil spills from shipping accidents, and the release of pollutants from vessel operations contribute to marine pollution. Antifouling paints used on ship hulls can release toxic substances into the water.

Effects of Marine Pollution:

1. **Impact on Marine Life:** Marine pollution can lead to the death and disruption of various marine species. Oil spills, for example, coat marine animals with oil, affecting their ability to swim, feed, and reproduce.

2. **Loss of Biodiversity:** The introduction of pollutants can disrupt the delicate balance of marine ecosystems, leading to the decline of certain species and the proliferation of others. This can result in a loss of biodiversity.

3. **Habitat Destruction:** Pollutants can degrade and destroy critical habitats such as coral reefs, mangroves, and seagrasses. These habitats are vital for the survival and reproduction of many marine species.

4. **Human Health Risks:** Contaminated seafood can pose health risks to humans who consume them. Accumulation of pollutants such as mercury and persistent organic pollutants in fish can lead to various health issues.

5. **Economic Impact:** Marine pollution can negatively impact fisheries, tourism, and coastal communities. Oil spills, for example, can lead to the death of fish stocks, affecting the livelihoods of those dependent on fishing.

Solutions to Marine Pollution:

1. **Regulatory Measures:** Implementation and enforcement of stringent regulations to control and monitor pollution sources, including oil spills, industrial discharges, and shipping activities.

2. **Waste Management:** Improved waste management practices on land can prevent the entry of plastics and other pollutants into the oceans. Recycling and proper disposal of waste are essential.

3. **Alternative Technologies:** The development and adoption of cleaner technologies in industries and shipping can reduce the release of pollutants into marine environments.

4. **International Cooperation:** Collaborative efforts among nations are crucial to address the global nature of marine pollution. Agreements and conventions, such as the MARPOL Convention, aim to regulate maritime pollution on an international scale.

5. **Public Awareness:** Raising awareness about the consequences of marine pollution through education campaigns can encourage responsible behaviour and promote a sense of stewardship towards the oceans.

6. **Research and Monitoring:** Continued research on the impacts of pollution and the development of innovative solutions are essential. Monitoring programs can help assess the effectiveness of pollution control measures.

Marine pollution requires a comprehensive and coordinated effort at local, national, and international levels. By implementing effective measures, raising awareness, and promoting sustainable practices, we can work towards preserving the health and vitality of our oceans for future generations.

Legislative measures related to water pollution control in India:

1. **Water (Prevention and Control of Pollution) Act, 1974:** This act is a key legislation aimed at preventing and controlling water pollution. It establishes boards for the prevention and control of water pollution at the central and state levels. The act empowers these boards to lay down standards for the quality of water, establish water quality monitoring networks, and take measures to prevent and control water pollution.

2. **Environment (Protection) Act, 1986:** The Environment Act provides a comprehensive legal framework for environmental protection in India. It grants the central government the authority to take measures to protect and improve the quality of the environment. Under this act, the Central Pollution Control Board (CPCB) is responsible for coordinating environmental protection activities.

3. **Water Cess Act, 1977:** The Water Cess Act allows for the levy and collection of a cess on water consumed by industries and local authorities. The funds collected are intended to be used for the prevention and control of water pollution.

4. **National Water Policy, 2012:** While not a legal act, the National Water Policy provides guidelines for the sustainable development and management of water resources in India. It emphasizes the need for pollution control and the promotion of water conservation and efficient use.

5. **River Boards Act, 1956:** The River Boards Act allows for the establishment of river boards to advise the central government on matters related to the regulation and development of inter-state rivers. These boards play a role in addressing issues related to water pollution in river systems.

6. **Biological Diversity Act, 2002:** This act is aimed at the conservation of biological diversity and sustainable use of its components. It includes provisions for preventing damage to biodiversity, which can be linked to water

pollution control efforts.

7. Forest (Conservation) Act, 1980: While primarily focused on forest conservation, this act indirectly contributes to water pollution control. Forests play a crucial role in maintaining watershed areas, preventing soil erosion, and ensuring the quality of water bodies.

8. The Graded Response Action Plan (GRAP): While not an act, GRAP is a set of emergency measures implemented in regions with poor air quality, which often includes measures related to water use and pollution control.

Soil Pollution

Soil pollution refers to the contamination of the Earth's soil with harmful substances, disrupting its natural composition and affecting its fertility, structure, and overall health. This type of pollution results from the introduction of pollutants, including chemicals, heavy metals, pesticides, and hazardous waste, into the soil through various human activities and industrial processes.

Soil pollution, an escalating environmental concern, unfolds as the insidious contamination of Earth's terrestrial skin. Resulting from human activities like industrial discharge, agricultural practices, and improper waste disposal, inflict lasting damage to ecosystems and human health. As anthropogenic agents infiltrate the soil, persistent pollutants disrupt the delicate balance, leading to dire consequences. Soil pollution jeopardizes agricultural productivity, seeps into groundwater, and poses severe health risks. Mitigating this menace demands a profound understanding of its causes, consequences, and sustainable solutions, ushering us into an era where soil preservation is paramount for the well-being of our planet.

3.3.1 Causes and Consequences of Soil Pollution:

Anthropogenic Activities:

1. Industrial Discharge:

Chemical Releases: Factories often release pollutants like heavy metals and industrial chemicals into the soil.

Waste Dumping: Improper disposal of industrial waste contributes to soil contamination.

2. Agricultural Practices:

Pesticides and Fertilizers: The use of agrochemicals, including pesticides and fertilizers, can lead to soil pollution.

Monoculture: Planting the same crop repeatedly depletes specific nutrients and increases vulnerability to pests.

3. Improper Waste Disposal:

Landfills: Dumping of municipal solid waste in landfills can result in the contamination of nearby soil.

Hazardous Waste: Incorrect disposal of hazardous waste poses a significant threat to soil quality.

Ecological and Health Consequences:

1. Ecosystem Impact:

Biodiversity Loss: Soil pollution can harm soil-dwelling organisms, affecting the overall biodiversity of an area.

Disruption of Nutrient Cycling: Contaminants can disrupt nutrient cycles essential for plant growth.

2. Agricultural Productivity:

Reduced Crop Yield: Soil pollution can lead to a decline in agricultural productivity due to nutrient imbalances and toxic effects on plants.

Food Chain Contamination: Contaminated soil may lead to the accumulation of pollutants in the food chain.

3. Human Health:

Contaminated Food: Consumption of crops grown in polluted soil can expose humans to harmful substances.

Groundwater Contamination: Persistent pollutants in soil may leach into groundwater, affecting drinking water quality.

3.3.2 Soil Quality Assessment:

Soil Testing:

Soil Sampling: Collecting representative soil samples from various locations for analysis.

Laboratory Analysis: Testing for parameters such as pH, nutrient content, heavy metals, and organic matter.

Interpretation of Results: Assessing soil health based on analysis results and recommending appropriate interventions.

Importance of Regular Soil Testing:

Sustainable Agriculture: Helps farmers optimize fertilizer use, leading to more efficient and sustainable agricultural practices.

Preventing Pollution: Early detection of soil pollution allows for timely remediation and preventive measures.

3.3.3 Soil Conservation Practices in India:

Sustainable Agriculture:

1. Organic Farming:

a. No Chemical Inputs:

Principles: Avoids synthetic fertilizers and pesticides, relying on natural alternatives. Promotes soil health by preserving microbial activity and biodiversity.

Soil Health: Enhances soil fertility and structure over time. Reduces the risk of chemical residue accumulation.

b. Crop Rotation:

Nutrient Cycling: Involves planting different crops in sequential seasons. Enhances nutrient cycling, reducing the need for external inputs.

Disease Control: Minimizes soil-borne diseases as different crops attract varying pests and pathogens. Breaks pest life cycles naturally.

2. Agroforestry:

a. Tree-Crop Integration:

Improved Soil Structure: Trees contribute organic matter through leaf litter, enhancing soil structure. The root systems of trees help bind soil particles, preventing erosion.

Diversification: Diverse tree-crop combinations enhance biodiversity, providing habitat for beneficial organisms. Increases resilience against pests and diseases.

b. Erosion Control:

Root System Impact: Tree roots anchor the soil, reducing surface runoff and erosion. Particularly effective on slopes and in areas prone to soil displacement.

Water Regulation: Improves water infiltration, reducing the risk of water-induced erosion. Stabilizes soil against extreme weather events.

3. Conservation Tillage:

a. Reduced Soil Disturbance:

Minimum Tillage: Involves minimal disruption of soil during planting and cultivation. Preserves soil structure and minimizes nutrient loss.

Benefits for Microorganisms: Protects soil-dwelling organisms and their habitats. Encourages beneficial microbial activity.

b. Water Conservation: Improved Water Retention: Maintains a more porous soil structure, enhancing water retention. Reduces water runoff, contributing to sustainable water use.

Climate Resilience: Mitigates the impact of drought by maintaining soil moisture. Adaptable to changing climate conditions.

Integration of Practices:

Synergy: Combining organic farming, agroforestry, and conservation tillage creates a synergistic effect. Enhances overall sustainability and resilience of agricultural systems.

Long-Term Impact: Cumulative benefits over time, such as improved soil fertility, reduced reliance on external inputs, and increased farm resilience. Supports the transition to more sustainable and regenerative agricultural practices.

Community and Economic Aspects: Community-based initiatives that promote these practices contribute to local economies. Increased consumer awareness and demand for sustainably produced food products.

Challenges and Considerations:

Transition Period: Challenges during the transition from conventional to sustainable practices. Education and support for farmers to navigate the initial stages.

Market Demand: Addressing market demand for sustainably produced goods. Building awareness among consumers about the benefits of sustainable practices.

Policy Support: The role of government policies in incentivizing and supporting sustainable agriculture. Encouraging and facilitating the adoption of sustainable practices through policy frameworks.

Soil Pollution Remediation Techniques: Bioremediation and Phytoremediation

1. Bioremediation:

a. Microbial Action:

Mechanism: Utilizes microorganisms such as bacteria, fungi, or algae. Microbes break down or neutralize pollutants through metabolic processes.

Applications: Effective against organic pollutants like hydrocarbons, pesticides, and certain industrial chemicals. Commonly applied in oil spill clean-ups and treatment of contaminated soils.

b. Enhanced Bioremediation:

Stimulation of Microbial Activity: Introduction of nutrients or amendments to enhance microbial growth. Accelerates the degradation of pollutants for faster remediation.

Applications: Applied in sites with slow or limited natural microbial activity. Useful for treating large-scale contamination in industrial areas.

2. Phytoremediation:

a. Plant-Based Clean-up:

Mechanism: Involves using plants to absorb, accumulate, or transform pollutants. Plants enhance the degradation or immobilization of contaminants through their root systems.

Applications: Effective for heavy metals, radioactive elements, and organic pollutants. Used in areas with moderate contamination, where plant growth is viable.

b. Hyperaccumulating Plants:

Characteristic Plants: Certain plant species exhibit hyperaccumulation, accumulating high levels of specific pollutants. Examples include ferns, willows, and sunflowers for different contaminants.

Applications: Suitable for soils with concentrated pollutants, especially heavy metals. Provides a sustainable approach to pollutant removal.

Applications in Mitigating Soil Pollution:

a. Industrial Sites:

Contaminants Addressed: Targets various industrial pollutants like heavy metals, solvents, and hydrocarbons.

Implementation: Applied during or after industrial operations to remediate soil. Common in brownfield redevelopment projects.

b. Agricultural Land:

Pollutants Tackled: Addresses agricultural contaminants such as pesticides, herbicides, and nutrient excess.

Implementation: Used to restore soil health in farmlands affected by chemical residues. A sustainable approach to reduce the environmental impact of agriculture.

Challenges and Considerations:

Site-specific Nature: Effectiveness depends on the type and concentration of pollutants. Tailored approaches are necessary for diverse contaminants.

Time Frame: Remediation may be time-consuming, especially for extensive pollution. Continuous monitoring and management are essential.

Ecological Impact: Assessing potential impacts on local ecosystems during and after remediation. Balancing the benefits of remediation with potential ecological disruptions.

Regulatory Compliance: Adhering to environmental regulations and obtaining necessary approvals. Collaboration with regulatory bodies for adherence to guidelines.

Understanding the causes and consequences of soil pollution, implementing soil quality assessment practices, and adopting conservation and remediation technologies are essential for sustainable land management and environmental health.

Effects of Soil Pollution

Sr No.	Type of effect	Example/Description
1	**Environmental Impact**	• Equilibrium of flora and fauna residing in the soil i.e. ecological system is disrupted. • Decreased nitrogen fixation. Formation of toxic dust, the foul odour of which is inconvenient to the people. • Increased waste has led to increased landfills, burning of these wastes or garbage then results in air pollution. • Irregular rainfall and flash floods due to soil erosion.
2	**Effect on Animal**	• Due to soil pollution natural environment and habitat gets damaged badly causing movement of some of the animal and bird species to new regions and sometimes these changes may be lethal to them. • Several species are pushed to the boundary of disappearance, due to no native land. Soil pollution may cause loss of several organisms residing in soil, ex. Earthworms leading to changes in the soil structure.
3	**Effect on Human**	• **Skin cancer and problems related to the human respiratory system.** • Chronic exposure to contaminated soil affects the genetic constitution of the body leading to congenital disease and chronic health ailments. **Mercury deposited in the soil can increase the risk of kidney damage. Headaches, eye irritation and skin rash.** • Long-term exposure to heavy metals, petroleum, solvents and agricultural chemicals can be carcinogenic. • Exposure to benzene for a longer period is linked with a higher occurrence of leukaemia.
4	**Industrial Effect**	• This is a severe problem in areas where industries directly discharge their wastes. These wastes may be more injurious to the soil as well as to humans when they have heavy metal compounds, asbestos, lead, organic compounds etc. • Hazardous chemicals discharged from industries that enter into underground water may cause ecological imbalance; release of pollutant gases that is air pollution, increased salinity, and reduced vegetation.
5	**Global Warming**	• Deforestation causes soil erosion which results in soil pollution leading to a disturbance in the balance of oxygen and carbon dioxide in the atmosphere causing an increase in temperature that is Global Warming.

Effects of Soil Pollution

Legislative measures related to soil protection and pollution control in India:

1. Water (Prevention and Control of Pollution) Act, 1974: While primarily focused on water pollution, this act also addresses pollution control in general. Contamination of water bodies can lead to soil pollution, and the act empowers pollution control boards to take measures to prevent and control such pollution.

2. Environment (Protection) Act, 1986: The Environment Act serves as a broad legal framework for environmental protection in India. It grants the central government the authority to take measures for the protection and improvement of the environment. Under this act, the Central Pollution Control Board (CPCB) has been established to coordinate environmental protection activities.

3. Forest (Conservation) Act, 1980: The Forest Act, while primarily focused on forest conservation, indirectly contributes to soil protection. Forests play a crucial role in maintaining soil fertility, preventing erosion, and promoting biodiversity.

4. National Environment Policy, 2006: The National Environment Policy provides a framework for sustainable development and addresses various environmental issues, including soil conservation and sustainable land use practices.

5. Solid Waste Management Rules, 2016: These rules under the Environment (Protection) Act provide guidelines for the management and handling of solid waste, including hazardous waste. Proper disposal of hazardous waste is critical to preventing soil pollution.

6. Biomedical Waste Management Rules, 2016: These rules aim to regulate the management and handling of biomedical waste, which, if not managed properly, can pose a threat to soil and water quality.

References:

1. Johnson, A., & Williams, B. (2010). Air quality standards and policies in India. Environmental Science Journal, 15(3), 102-115.
2. Gupta, S., & Singh, M. (2019). Soil pollution and its impact on agriculture. Journal of Environmental Science, 25(4), 567-580.
3. Miller, T., & Smith, R. (2018). Environmental Challenges: Causes, Consequences, and Solutions. London: Green Press.
4. Patel, K. N. (2015). Water Pollution in Developing Countries. Mumbai: Eco Awareness Publishers.

As we conclude this exploration into the realms of environmental science, let us not merely close the book but embark on a journey of continued learning and conscientious action. The insights shared within these pages are a stepping stone, not a destination, and I invite you to carry the spirit of inquiry and responsibility forward.

1. Additional Resources: For those seeking further knowledge, a curated list of additional resources, books, and websites awaits. Dive deeper into specific topics and stay informed about the latest developments in environmental science.

2. References: Acknowledging the wealth of knowledge that informs this book, the references section provides a comprehensive list of sources. Delve into the works of scientists, researchers, and advocates who have contributed to our understanding of the environment.

4. Index: An index is provided for quick reference, enabling readers to locate specific topics, concepts, and discussions throughout the book. Use it as a guide to revisit and explore key themes at your convenience.

5. Beyond the Pages: In this final section, the author shares reflections on the journey undertaken in crafting this book. Gain insight into the motivations, challenges, and inspirations that shaped the narrative, connecting on a more personal level with the storyteller behind the science.

As we close this chapter, may the knowledge gained be a catalyst for informed choices, sustainable practices, and a renewed commitment to preserving the intricate beauty of our planet. The story of our environment is ongoing, and your role as a steward is integral to its unfolding.

Thank you for joining me on this exploration.

Aishwarya Jain

"beyond The Pages"

As we conclude this environmental science journey, I extend my deepest gratitude to you, the reader, for embarking on this exploration. "Beyond the Pages" provides a window into the motivations, challenges, and inspirations that shaped the narrative of this book. Crafting this work has been a labour of love, fueled by a passion for understanding and preserving the delicate balance of our planet.

Environmental science is more than a field of study; it is a call to action. The challenges and opportunities it presents require collective effort, and your role as a reader is pivotal. Reflect on the insights gained, consider the personal connections forged with the material, and contemplate your responsibility in nurturing a sustainable future.

I hope this book has ignited a spark of curiosity, a sense of wonder, and a commitment to conscientious living. The story of our environment is ongoing, and each of us contributes to its narrative. As you turn the final page, remember that the journey continues, not just within these chapters, but in your choices, actions, and the legacy you leave for generations to come.

Thank you for being a part of this exploration.

With gratitude,

Aishwarya Jain

www.ingramcontent.com/pod-product-compliance
Ingram Content Group UK Ltd.
Pitfield, Milton Keynes, MK11 3LW, UK
UKHW062008290726
14090UKWH00022B/1458